LEARN HOW TO MAKE CONTACT WITH BENEVOLENT ALIENS

A Guidebook on Humanity's Consciousness Evolutionary Leap

Dedication

This book is dedicated to my Star Family Beings that are patiently helping and guiding me through my awakenings and navigating this 3D planet to ascend into 5D and beyond.
Thank you!!!

Questions, Comments, & Media Collaborations
5dlifenow@gmail.com
www.5dlifenow.co
@5DLIFENOW

Terms

The book utilizes the free fair use public work agreement on written and graphic works. Please view each of the references for the image source of content. For legal purposes I must state this is for entertainment purposes only. Use at your own risk, I do not guarantee or warranty anything. I will not be held liable for any legal disputes as all this information is freely available online. I encourage you to do your own research.

I am divinely protected as you are too. So it is.

LEARN HOW TO MAKE CONTACT WITH BENEVOLENT ALIENS

Note from the Author

The Aliens made me write this 😂
In all seriousness, they told me that humans need to know what our abilities are, how to use them, and most importantly how to properly and safely communicate with other multidimensional beings for the <u>safety of all involved</u>.

We humans don't know our true full potential power yet and are coming in too hot and toxic. We don't realize it yet but we can physically harm other beings just with our thoughts and vibration alone. In this book, you'll learn how to attune your mind, body, and energy to the ideal setting for safe, joyous, and incredible interdimensional communication.

When writing books I always use divine guidance and gain advice from my Star Family. I probably could have made this book three times as long but I'm often nudged to keep it simple and if the readers have questions they can easily research it online or contact me for more info.

LEARN HOW TO MAKE CONTACT WITH BENEVOLENT ALIENS

Foreword

This is not your average type of booklet. This booklet has channeled messages, quantum information, and light codes embedded into the energetic sequence of the words, images, and pages.

Some of it is center line formatted to center the focus of your mind. Much of the wording and formatting is intentionally different from the standard so as to surprise the amygdala in the brain, allowing for the information to penetrate deeper into the subconscious. It is also written with real life examples, references, resources, and exercises to help further your abilities, expand your consciousness and activate your DNA.

Say: I am divinely guided with love on my soul journey and am fully protected in the highest vibration of crystalline love ✨

Table of Contents

Introduction

6 Steps to Make Contact

7 Prepping Steps

Intention

1 Cosmic Web

Collective Consciousness

18+ Dimensions

7+ Light Body

3 Types & 34 Names of Aliens

22 Psychic Abilities

7 Layers of Attunement

30 Ways of Communication

Galactic Etiquette

12+ Exercises

35+ Resources

References

About the Author

Introduction

Welcome to Learning How to Communicate with Benevolent Aliens. Surprisingly, you're more than likely already in contact with them and you don't even know it yet. The reality is, we all have a soul, Higher Self, Spirit, Spirit Guides, Ancestors, Star Family Beings, and Galactic supporters that are helping us right now.

We have all been incarcerated hundreds or thousands of times on this planet and most likely many other planets too. We've been all different genders and orientations of beings, humans, plants, animals, and even rocks. As most Indigenous cultures know, everything has a spirit. Our souls start out as a small first dimensional being and then we grow throughout many lifetimes on a wide variety of soul journeys. That's what life is about, the journey of our soul which is a fractal of the Universe (God) experiencing itself.

By reading this, you will deepen your connection to your divinity and progress your soul journey, along with learning how to communicate with our Alien / Star Being friends safely and respectfully.

Introduction

On December 21st, 2012, the Earth's axis shifted and our planet entered a gamma wave belt of higher dimensional energies. This is causing gamma radiation exposure which is activating 90% more of our DNA and neurological pathways. All of this is causing a chain reaction within humanity, especially throughout our DNA. We were created with 12 strands of DNA but between 9-10 strands we're "unhooked". The "dormant 90%" is now becoming activated and with this book you will increase that progression in yourself and the collective.

Finally, Earth Surface Humans can have greater access to our extra perception and sensory abilities for interaction with Aliens, Spirits, and many other Interdimensional Beings.

This is truly a magical time to be alive!
Let's dive in ✨

Steps to Make Contact

Step 1: Set Intention & Boundaries
Step 2: Learn Cosmic Knowledge
Step 3: Prep Your Body, Mind & Spirit
Step 4: Try Various Contact Methods
Step 5: Journal, reflect, & Evaluate
Step 6: Option to share your experiences

Not every step may be necessary for every person. Some people may have to go through the steps multiple times while others can skip ahead or jump between steps. No matter where you're at in your soul journey, that's exactly where you need to be.

Steps in Prepping Your Body, Mind & Spirit

Step 1: Intention
Step 2: Cosmic Understanding
Step 3: Attunement
Step 4: Shadow Work & Clearing
Step 5: Soul Journey
Step 6: Re-attunement
Step 7: Connection & Contact

This will create full awareness of your sense of self, the YOU-niverse, Source/God, and of course, other sentient beings. Everything is divinely connected and you once knew it all. By incarnating on earth you forget everything. Now is the time to remember who you really are, why you came here, and to step into your true power.

Intention

<u>Ask yourself these important questions:</u>

- Why do I want to make contact with Aliens?
- How will I react to an Alien in person?
- Will I get emotionally excited, scared, nervous?
- How do I think the Alien will react if it's a positive, very strange, and/or negative experience?

Firstly, it's important to note that we humans are VERY emotional dualistic beings - which is normal but, our vibration is so strong we affect everything around us. Emotions amplify our vibration which ripples out around us. Alien Star Beings are highly sensitive and sometimes our vibration can become too much for them or potentially worse, we could even harm them. It's critical, during all types of communication, to remain calm and be in a heart centered loving state. We have exponential power and unlimited abilities that we have very little knowledge of, so far.

By honing your abilities, setting your intention, and visualizing connecting with Star Beings in a positive loving calm state you're setting yourself up for the ideal contact conditions.

To set the vibrational tone for this guidebook, we must clear space for this beautiful new higher vibrational energy.

To do this we must release all past hurt, trauma, guilt, shame, toxins, parasites, parasitic attachments, and low vibrational feelings, thoughts, emotions, and energies. It's a lot of self work but is well worth it!

We now leave all of that behind to step forward on our ascension pathway to higher density realms through 4D and into 5D consciousness, also known as Christ Consciousness. Which is a pure loving vibrational state that we now intend on connecting with ONLY benevolent Star and Spirit Beings for the benefit of all involved.

Intention

As you are most likely aware at this point, it's important you bring your team in to help assist you along this journey.

"What? I have a team?" you ask. Yes! You have Spirit Guides, Guardian Angels, many other types of angels, Ancestors, Loved Ones, Spirit Animals, Nature Beings, your Star Family and even your future self - your Higher Self. If you have never connected with them, now is the time. Know that you have been divinely guided here to do so.

Say "I acknowledge my benevolent loving team that is helping guide me through this incarnation". They are typically always around you all the time, some humans have 3-6 or 10-20 Spirit Guides plus other beings depending on the person and their soul journey. You could have 50 or more though, everyone has a unique team and it's an absolute blessing to connect with them. They are very eager to connect with you and can only help assist you if you ask for it.

Say out loud, loudly, strong, and with purpose:

"I now allow my benevolent loving Spirit Guides, Star Beings, Ancestors, and Angels of light to fully aid me along my soul journey for my highest good.

I allow for contact in synchronicities, clairvoyant visions, in dream space, clairaudient messages, clairsentient feelings...for the highest good of all involved."

Be specific and tailor the wording to suit you. Be very careful with your wording and make sure you state that it's with benevolent loving beings that have high vibrational peaceful and loving intentions for all.

With the intention set, we must gain vital cosmic knowledge, learn about the cosmic web system, dimensions, types of Aliens & Star Beings, psychic abilities, how to attune your physical body, ways of communication, how to speak to them, what to say and do, what not to say, resources, and most importantly, practice!

You already have everything you need inside of you to communicate with Aliens and all beings - Animals, Plants, Elementals, Nature Spirits, Angels, God, Spirit Guides, and Ancestors.

Now for boundaries, you can tailor this how you like. I recommend stating:

"No being can possess me, nor can they take over my body. I do not allow for any interactions with low vibrational beings, entities, or spirits. So be it. I surround myself with pure crystalline loving white light energy."

Make sure when you're saying things out loud or in your mind they are with strong purpose and strong energy life force to make a defined energetic signal.

Cosmic Knowledge

The Cosmic Web

This is how everything is connected. It is physically represented by the woven fascia and muscles in our 3D human bodies. It is a webbing system that extends and expands throughout us, our cities, our planet, and out to every part of our universe and further into the multiverse. This is how we're all divinely connected.

No matter if you want to believe in this or not, it's there always and we're always connected in. Once you learn how to utilize your connection you can travel, communicate, and channel information through it. Close your eyes and connect with it now.

Cosmic Knowledge

The Collective Consciousness

In 2019, I began receiving visions of these strange etheric thought clouds that were attached to humans. I had no idea what I was being shown until later in 2020 after multiple intense awakenings and ET visitations during the "coco". I watched a video by Doenut Factory about Egregores and felt as if I left my body in amazement. I flashed back to a year prior when my Star Family showed me them.

Each thought we think creates a small electrically charged thought bubble when two or more people are thinking the same thought they create a mini egregore. When mass amounts of people are thinking the same thought it becomes a massive egregore.

All egregores together make up the human collective consciousness that is built into the Comic Web.

I was also shown how to basically hack into the collective consciousness to systematically update and raise the vibration of humanity. No pressure right?! Well, finally after a few years of researching, self discovery, and healing I'm finally sharing this vital information.

YOU, have the ability of connecting into the collective consciousness too. You can download and upload information from and, you are already unconsciously doing it without effort. Imagine putting effort in to it and what you can achieve. I encourage you to put more high vibrational love into the egregore systems.

Cosmic Knowledge
The Collective Consciousness

Just as we here on earth have a collective consciousness, there is also a Cosmic collective consciousness and endless other ET civilization collective consciousness's - Like RA. We as high powered multidimensional light beings have the ability to access each of the major and minor collective consciousness's via the Cosmic Web! How cool is that?

I'm amazed everyday by this and rarely get to share my excitement of the unbelievable universe we're in. Many humans already access different levels of consciousness through channeling, attuning to the right frequency, in dream space, astral travel, hypnotherapy, and through our many extraordinary etheric abilities.

All humans download and upload information to the human collective consciousness daily without even realizing it. Some people may not even want to accept this information but we're already all tied into it. Disconnection can happen through low vibrations, substance use, parasitic attachments, toxins, etc. That's another reason why it's so important to cleanse and clear the bodies (physical & energetic).

Awakening to the conscious awareness of your eternal soul and how you relate with the multidimensional Cosmic Web is essential in making intentional peaceful contact.

There are unlimited dimensions existing all around us simultaneously happening while we live our 3D lives. Up until this point so much of humanity's education, medical, and societal systems have focused primarily only on the physical body whilst completely negating the energetic bodies and other dimensional realms. These etheric elements are existing and affecting us whether we believe it or not. On the next page we go through the multidimensional map.

Part of the reason we can't see Aliens, Spacecrafts, Elementals, and non-human beings is because they are in higher dimensions.

Our eyes are limited with the light spectrum but sometimes our eyes may see other beings but our brain can't process the images so it filters them out. Right now, humans are evolving physically, energetically, and spiritually. This is your multidimensional invitation to explore beyond our physical senses.

Cosmic Knowledge

Dimensions

Universal Templar Complex, Spheres within Spheres

15-Dimensional Time Matrix
5 Density Universes (DU)

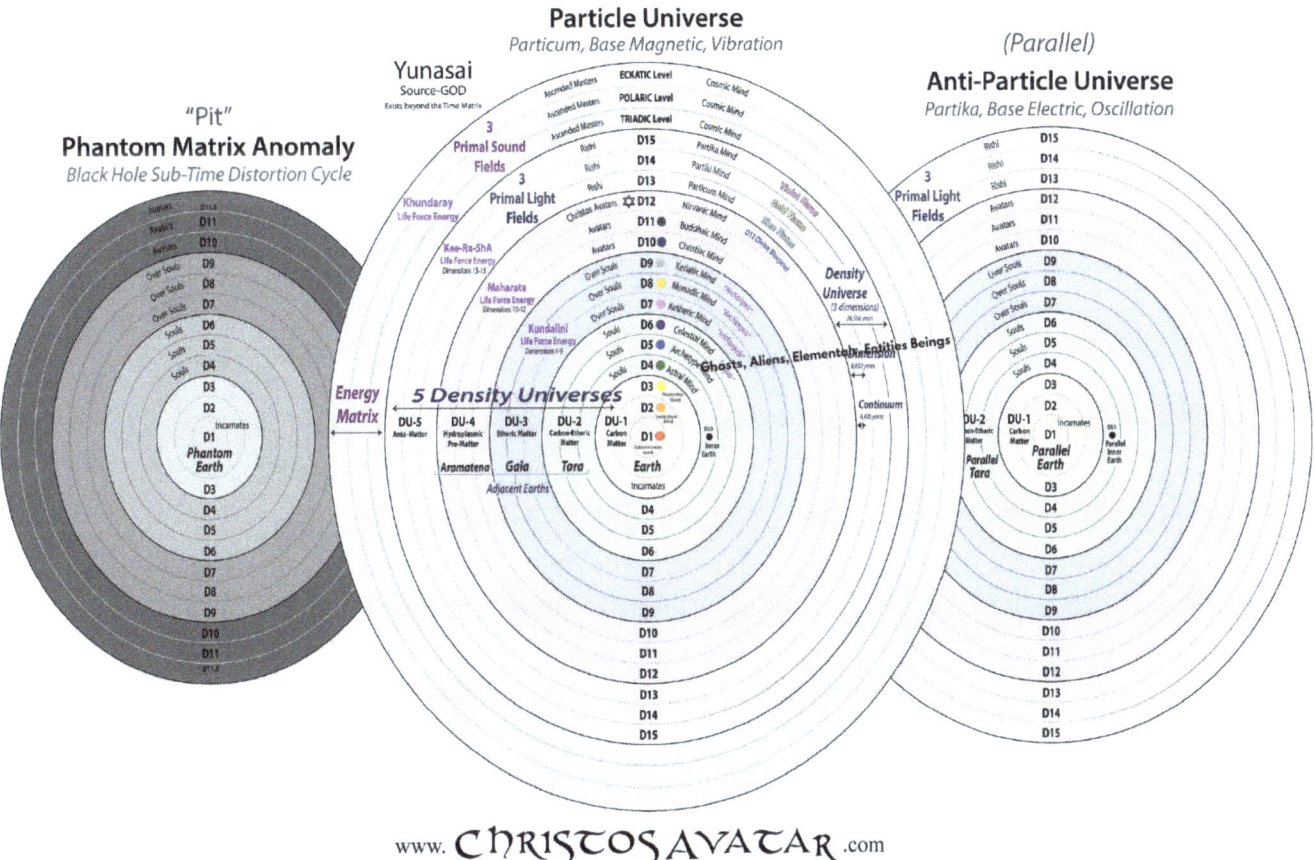

www.CHRISTOSAVATAR.com

There are a few different types of dimensional maps but I have found this one by Christos Avatar is well laid out and simple to mentally digest. If we don't know what a dimension is or that there are other ones all around us and other beings in them, we just don't know - might have suspicions - but what we have only been told, taught and shown in human life is only the 1st density of the 1st, 2nd and 3rd dimensions. I began my suspicions at age 7, I knew there was more. When I first saw this, I cried with joy. It's a confirmation of what I knew 30 years ago!

Humans are multidimensional beings living on a multidimensional planet in a multidimensional universe. We're going in and out of and existing on different levels and densities all the time. For example, when humans dream, the pineal gland releases melatonin and DMT that creates a multidimensional gateway for the astral body to detach from the physical body. The multidimensional gateway is connected to the Cosmic Web in the 4th dimension. From there, we have the ability to go virtually anywhere but to do that, one must become conscious in dream state which is called Lucid Dreaming - see the practice session to learn how.

Cosmic Knowledge
Dimensions

Within each dimension there are densities and unlimited subdimensions. Once you become skilled at Lucid Dreaming/Astral Projection, you can go into different dimensional states. Even when you daydream or feel "floaty" like you're not grounded and are out of your body. Some people call it "having a brain fart". You're really attuned into a different dimension. Just as we can tune into higher dimensions, we can tune into lower ones too. Check in to your body, where are you at? Check in more often to gain a sense of your frequency fluctuations each day.

Cosmic Knowledge
Dimensions

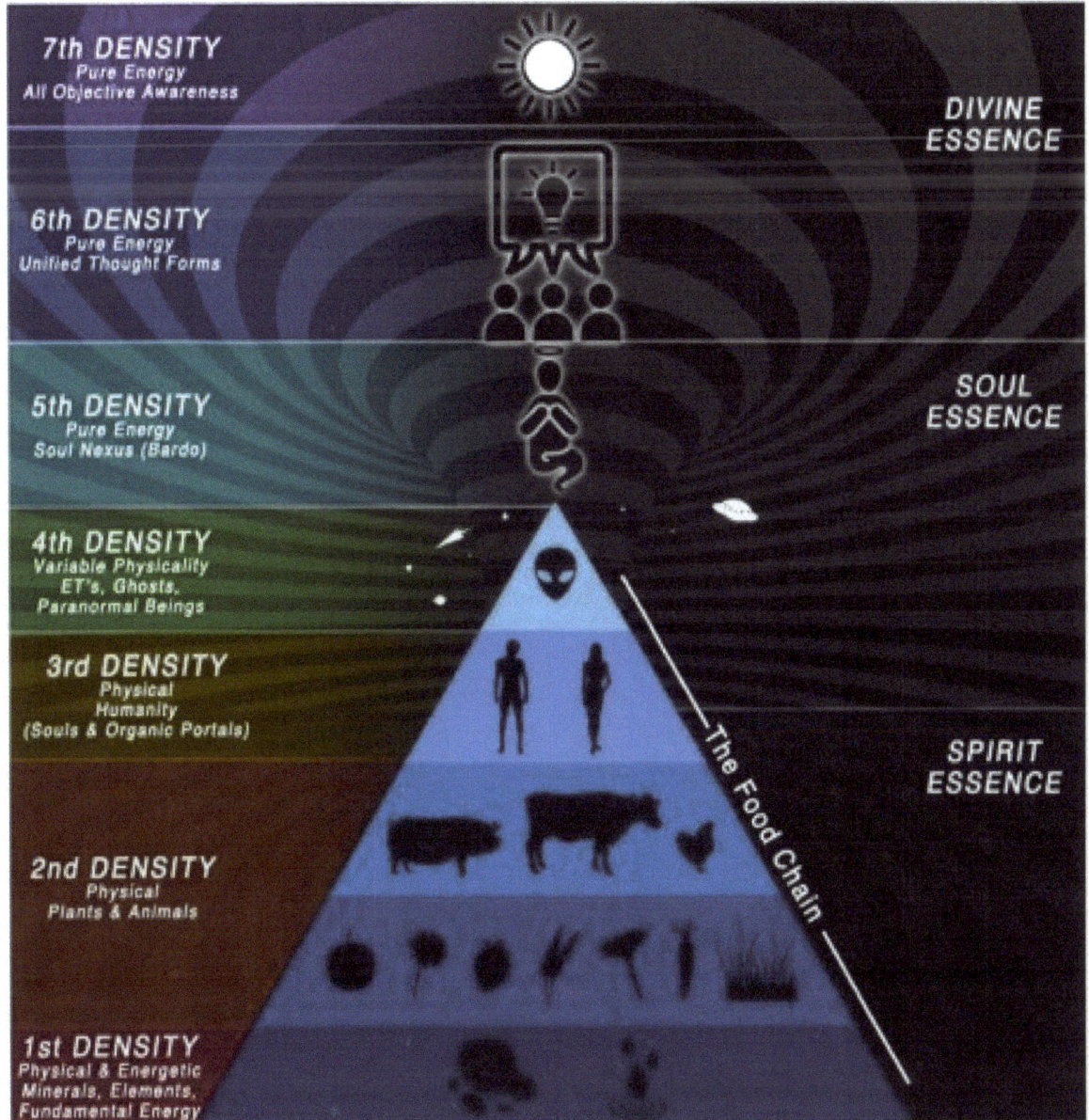

From each image and map you can see a slightly different perspective to help open your consciousness. Read each one carefully and with intention to help integrate the information deep into your mind and into the social memory complex of humanity. You'll notice, humans are not the top of the food chain. It's true there are carnivorous non-humans we share this earth with that eat humans. They're a mix of Reptilians, luciferians, Orion Greys, Nephalims, and insectoids. Everything has been kept from humanity so their secret food chain top position could stay safe. Well, not anymore!

Cosmic Knowledge

Dimensions

REALITIES DIMENSIONS / DENSITIES / LAYERS

8D	8TH DENSITY — NEW OCTAVE / INFINITY	INFINITY / NEW UNIVERSE? / NEW BIG BANG? / GOING BACK TO THE 1ST DENSITY?
7D	7TH DENSITY — GATEWAY / ONENESS	ONENESS / NO IDENTITY, NO PAST, NO FUTURE / EXISTING IN THE ALL / BLACK HOLES
6D	6TH DENSITY — PURE ENERGY UNIFIED	UNITY / "ANGELS" / DIVINE BEINGS / RA / UNIFIED MEMORY COMPLEX / HIGHER SELF
5D	5TH DENSITY — WISDOM / LIGHT	LOVE, BALANCE BETWEEN LIGHT / WISDOM / PURE LIGHT / IMMORTAL
4D	4TH DENSITY: ASTRAL PLANE	ET's / FRACTAL BEINGS / UNDERSTANDING / THOUGHT AND EMOTIONAL COMPLEXES
3D	3TH DENSITY: SELF-AWARENESS	PHYSICAL HUMANITY / SELF / CONSCIOUSNESS / AWARENESS BEGINS
2D	2ND DENSITY: GROWTH	PHYSICAL PLANTS & ANIMALS
1D	1ST DENSITY: BEINGNESS	BASIC ELEMENTS (WATER, AIR, FIRE, MINERALS, FUNDAMENTAL ENERGY ETC

Here's another similar map with slight variations. Try drawing, visualizing, and seeking each dimensional plain out during meditation and astral projection.

On the next page it explains how the physical human eyes can only perceive a small fraction of light energy. This is why it's crucial for us to develop our visualization and extrasensory abilities to be able to communicate with other types of sentient Beings.

Cosmic Knowledge
Dimensions

We open our eyes and we think we're seeing the whole world out there. But what has become clear is that when you look at the electro-magnetic spectrum we are seeing less than 1/10 billionth of the information that's riding on there. So we call that "visible light". But everything else passing through our bodies is completely invisible to us. Even though we accept reality that's presented to us, we are really only seeing a little window of what's happening.

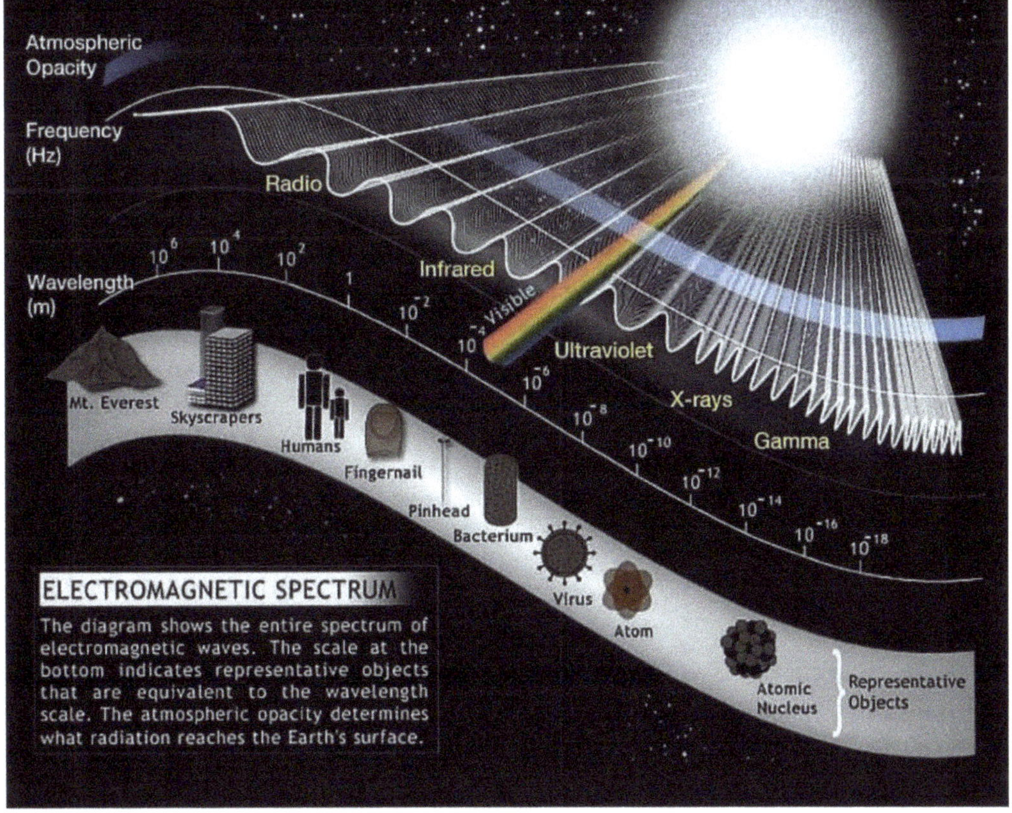

ELECTROMAGNETIC SPECTRUM

The diagram shows the entire spectrum of electromagnetic waves. The scale at the bottom indicates representative objects that are equivalent to the wavelength scale. The atmospheric opacity determines what radiation reaches the Earth's surface.

Light is Consciousness

The visible spectrum is the portion of the electromagnetic spectrum that is visible to the human eye. Electromagnetic radiation in this range of wavelengths is called visible light or simply light. A typical human eye will respond to wavelengths from about 380 to 740 nanometers. In terms of frequency, this corresponds to a band in the vicinity of 430–770 Terahertz (THz).

Cosmic Knowledge
Dimensions

These are two other diagrams of the light spectrum which most humans can only see a limited amount compared to what is really happening around us.

What we see and have been trained to focus on is located in the 1st, 2nd, and 3rd dimensions only (i.e.: 1st density). The 4th, 5th, and higher dimensions are also occurring all around and inside of us too - even though we can't physically see it, it's still happening.

As you learn how to attune yourself to higher dimensions you will learn how to use your etheric extrasensory abilities to tap into much more of our reality.

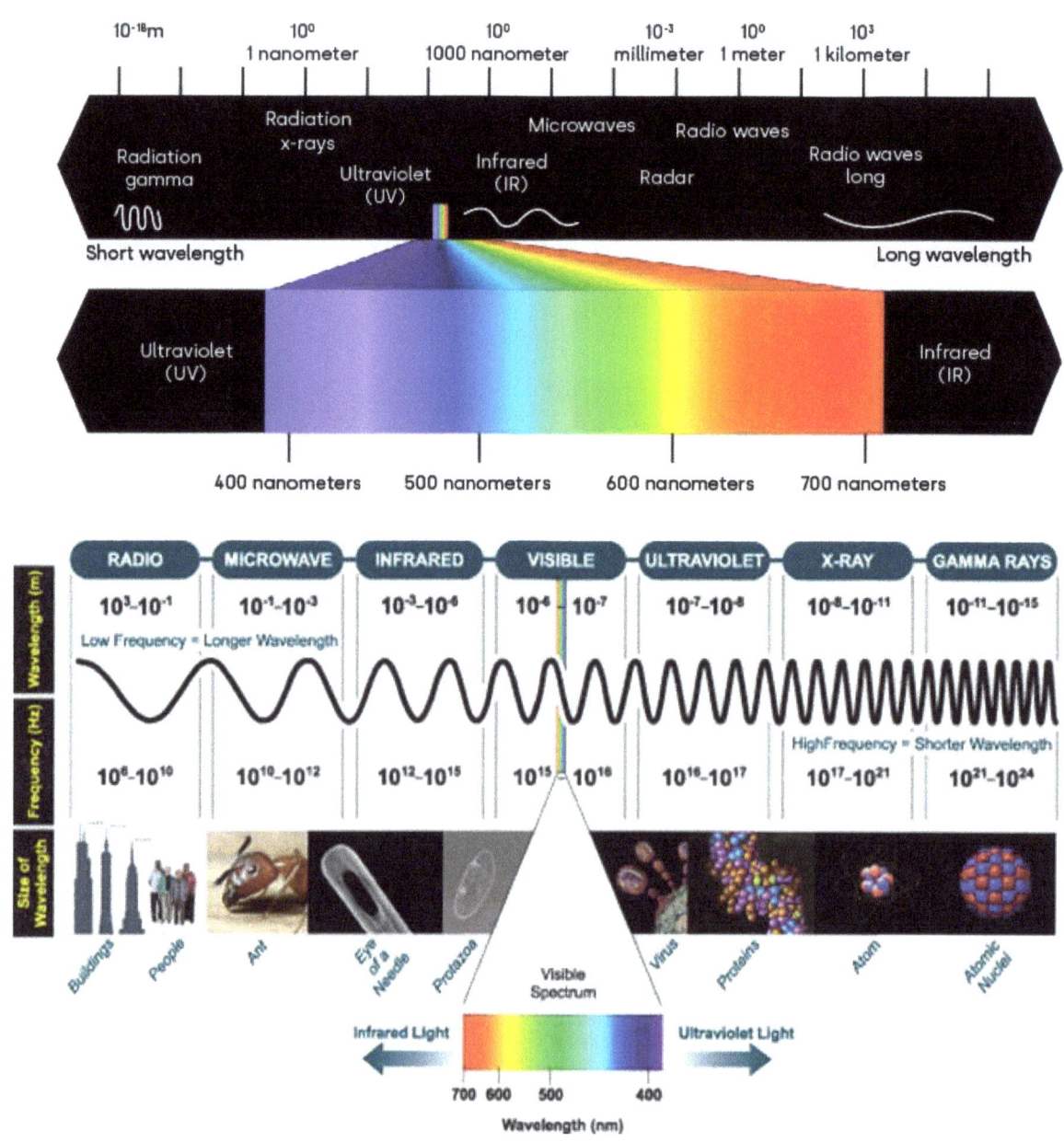

Cosmic Knowledge
Dimensions

This is the Tree of Life. There's so much to unpack and explain in this but that will have to be for another book. I feel compelled to include it in here and if you so choose go and do your research on it, it is well worth it! Spirit Science has excellent videos on it for free on YouTube.

Cosmic Knowledge
Dimensions

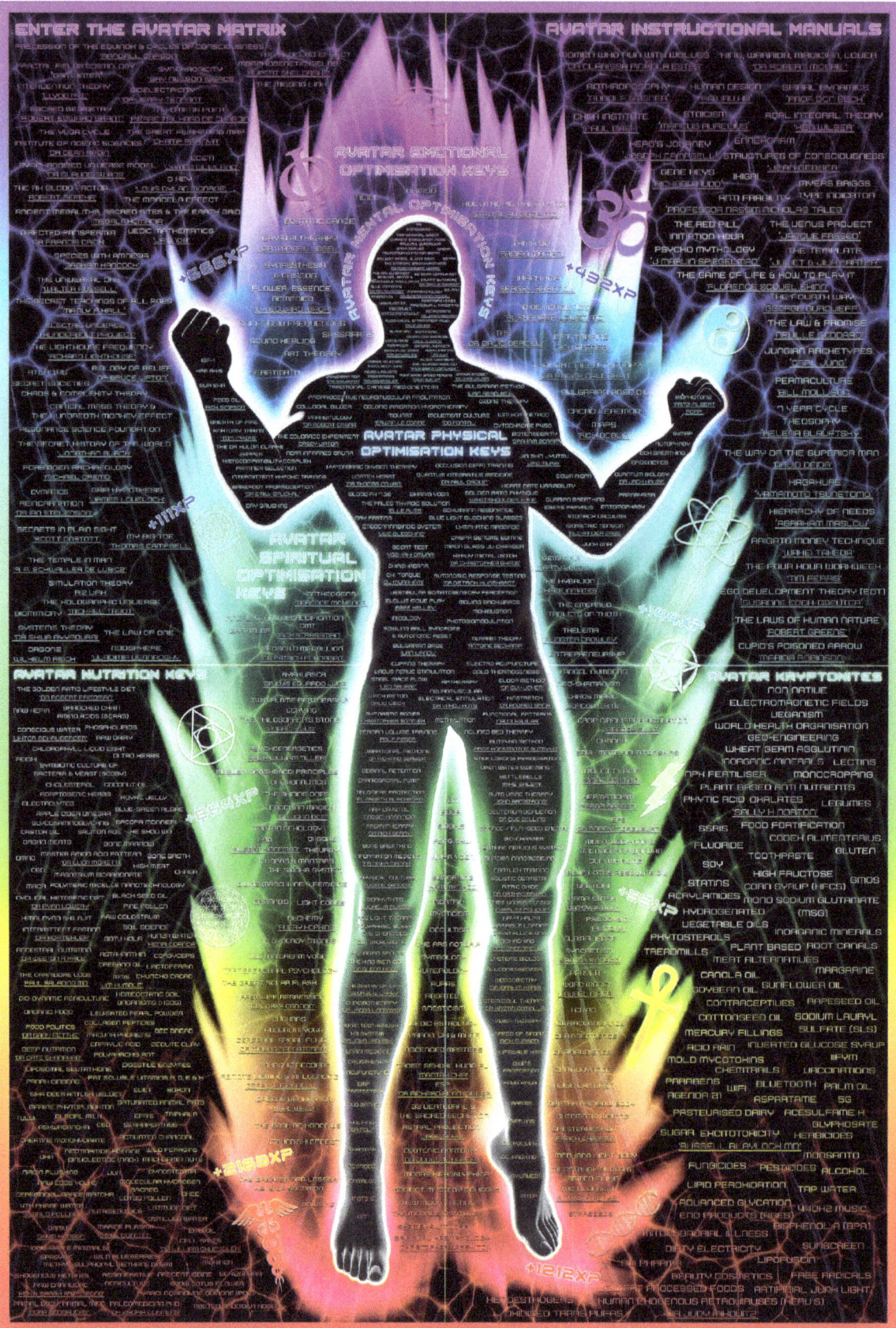

Keys to upgrading your human avatar body. Yes, it can be a bit overwhelming but take your time and do what you feel you're being guided to. Your body knows exactly what it needs to progress.

Cosmic Knowledge
Dimensions

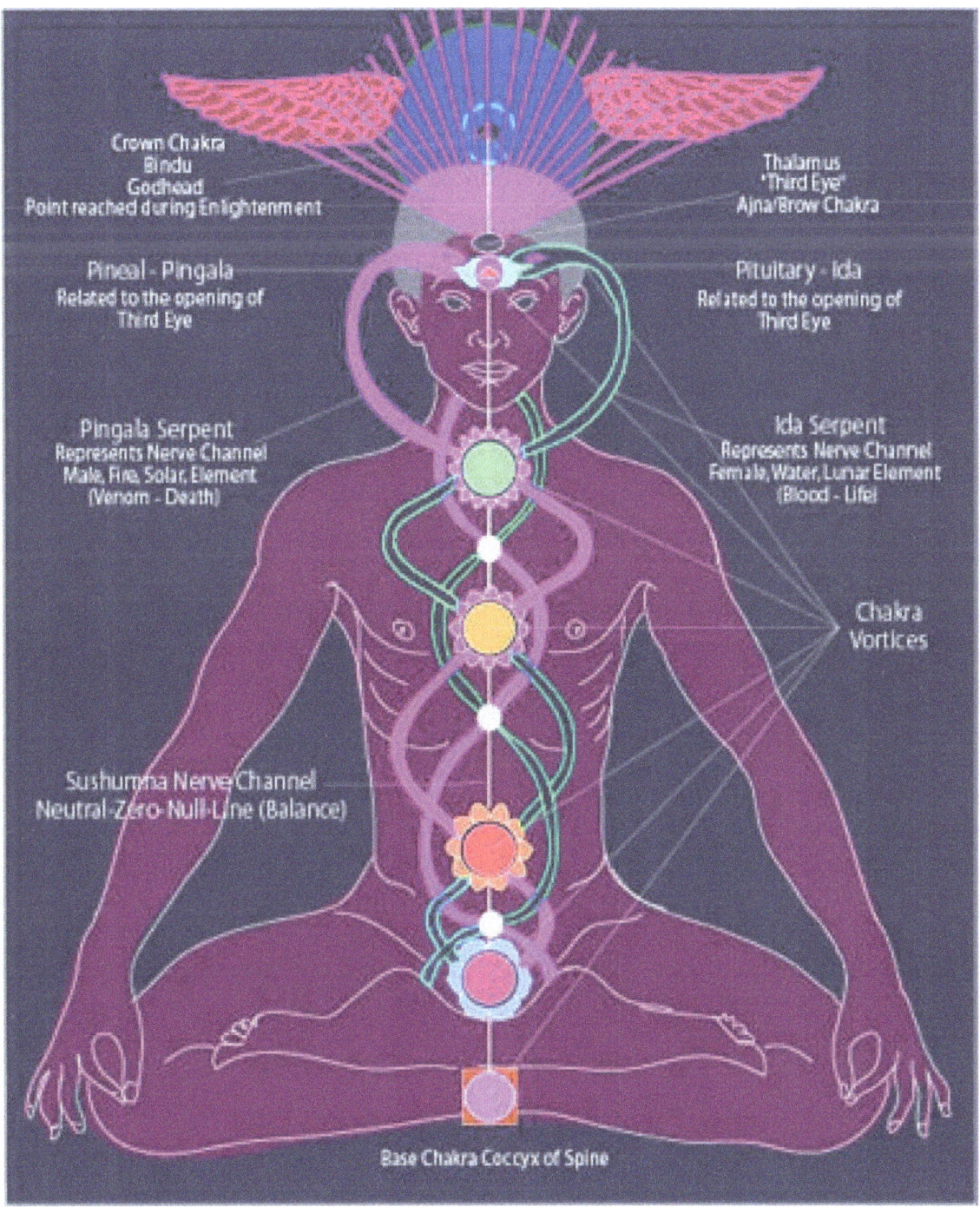

This is an excellent visual of the rising up of Kundalini energy in the Chakras and up the spine. I can do this in my meditations quite easily now and often feel the energy rise up and twirl my body around in a spinning motion while seated. An easy way to achieve this is by doing Dr. Joe Dispenza's Brain & Heart Coherence Meditations for at least 3 months - it is the gateway into 5D consciousness.

Cosmic Knowledge
Light Body

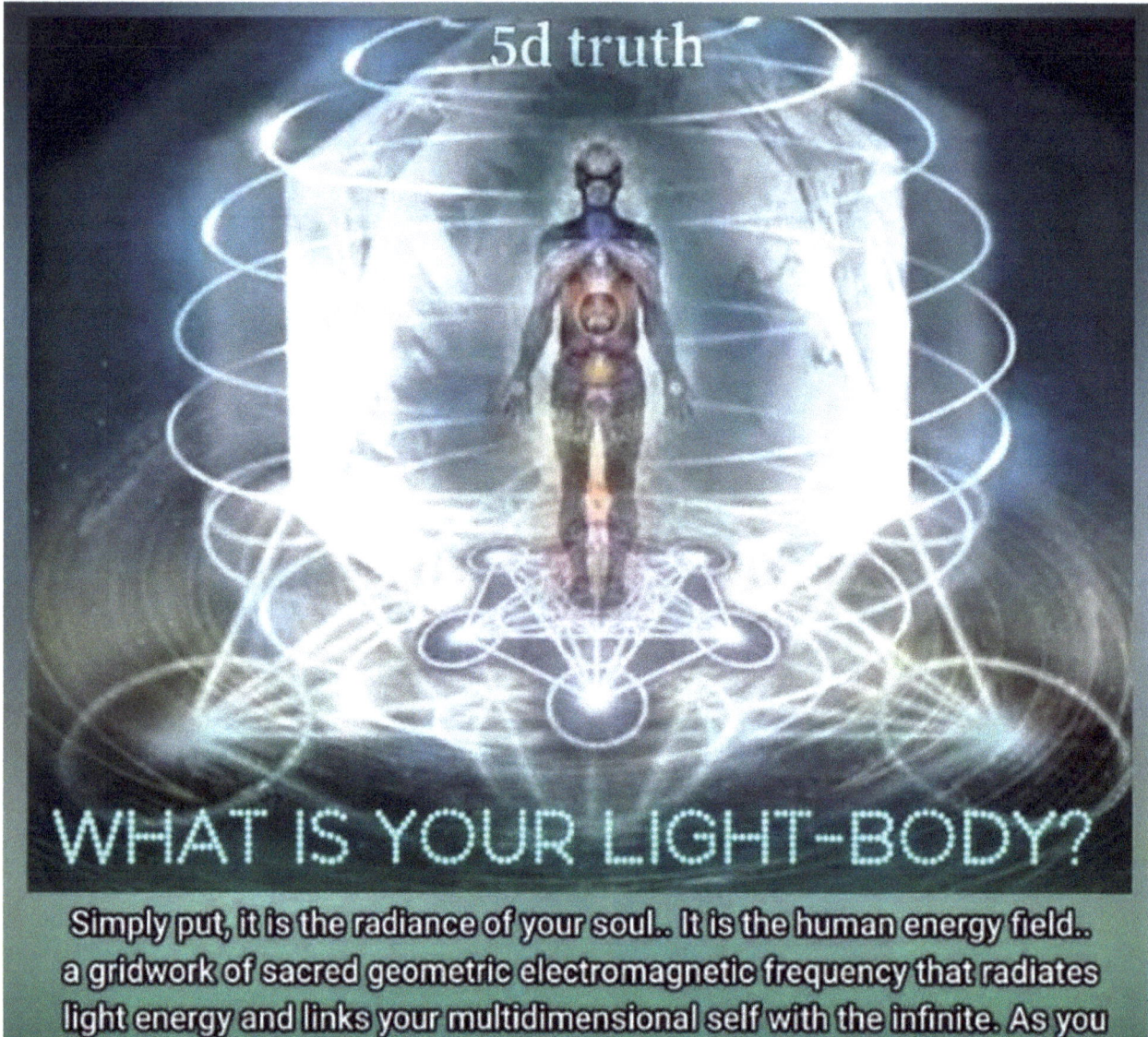

You are not just your physical body. You have multiple bodies made up of light energy that our physical eyes are not able to see, yet. As we evolve, we will become more aware and attuned to our light bodies that extend throughout our physical body. It's important to tap into your energetic body everyday to further connect and feel it. Disease always starts in the energy level first before the physical. You have the ability to clear any toxic disease energy and heal yourself along with others too.

Cosmic Knowledge
Light Body

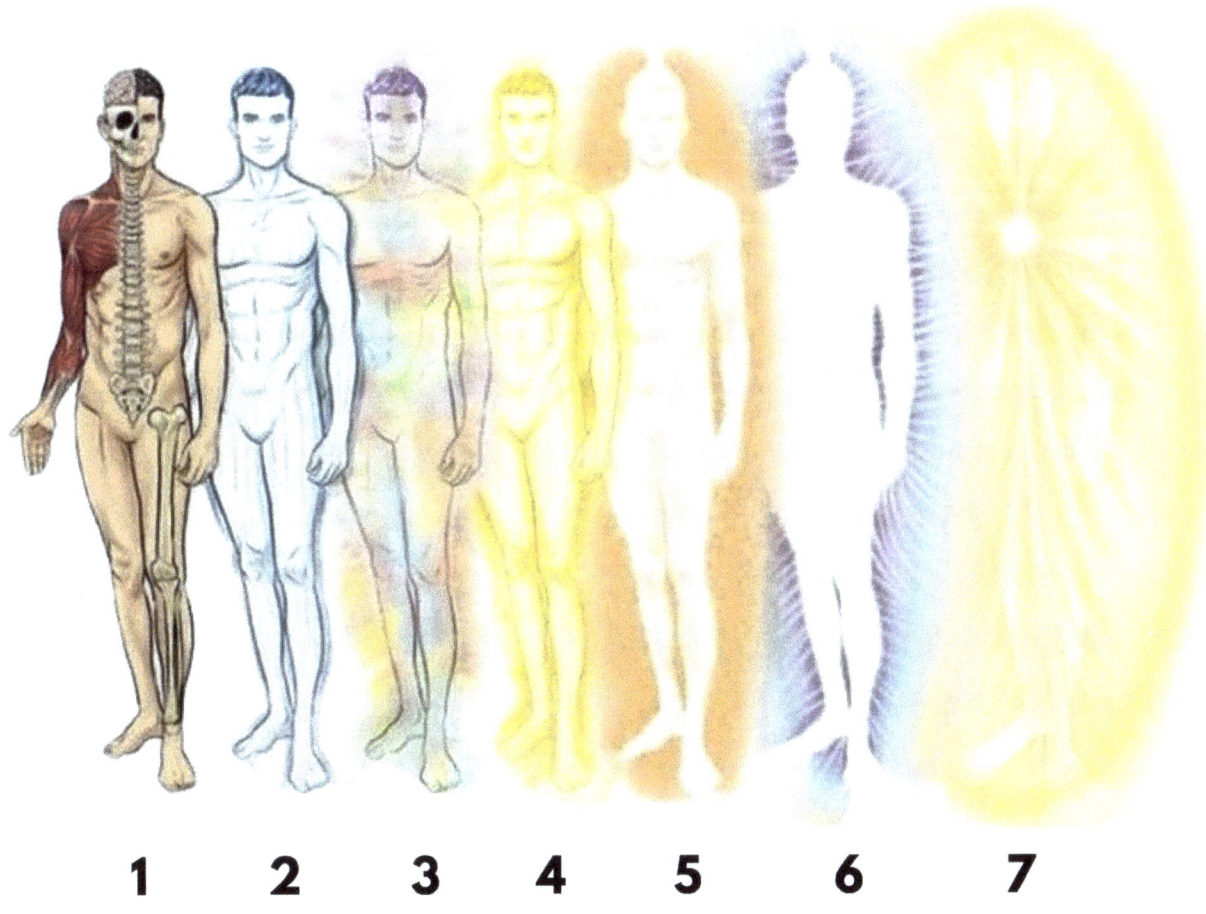

Just like we have layers of our skin and physical body tissues, we have layers of our energetic bodies. Going from left to right:

1.   **Physical Body**
2.   **Etheric Body**
3.   **Astral Body**
4.   **Mental Body**
5.   **Casual Body**
6.   **Buddhi Body**
7.   **Athma Body**

Each one could have its own book, if you're drawn to one or more I encourage you to do your research on it and become consciously aware of your energy layers.

Cosmic Knowledge

Light Body

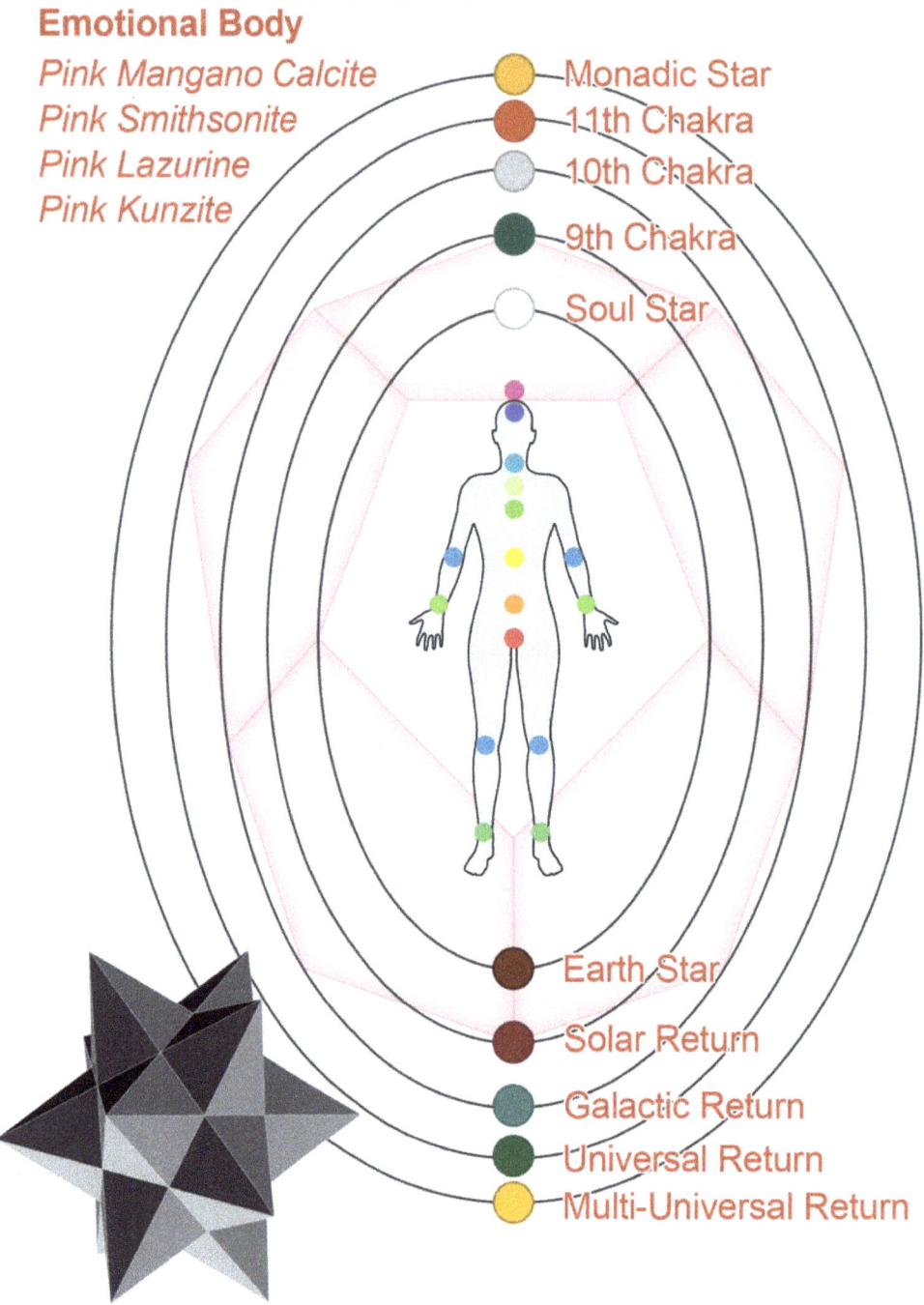

Pink Stellated Dodecahedron
Emotional Body

Pink Mangano Calcite
Pink Smithsonite
Pink Lazurine
Pink Kunzite

- Monadic Star
- 11th Chakra
- 10th Chakra
- 9th Chakra
- Soul Star
- Earth Star
- Solar Return
- Galactic Return
- Universal Return
- Multi-Universal Return

Our energy bodies extend far out beyond our physical body, to our Higher Self and Cosmic Self. This is a simplified diagram showing our external and even further out Chakra energy points. Stop, take a moment to regard this deeply and let it sink into your subconscious to activate your higher conscious memory. Now, take a moment to realize we truly amazing beings!

Cosmic Knowledge
Light Body

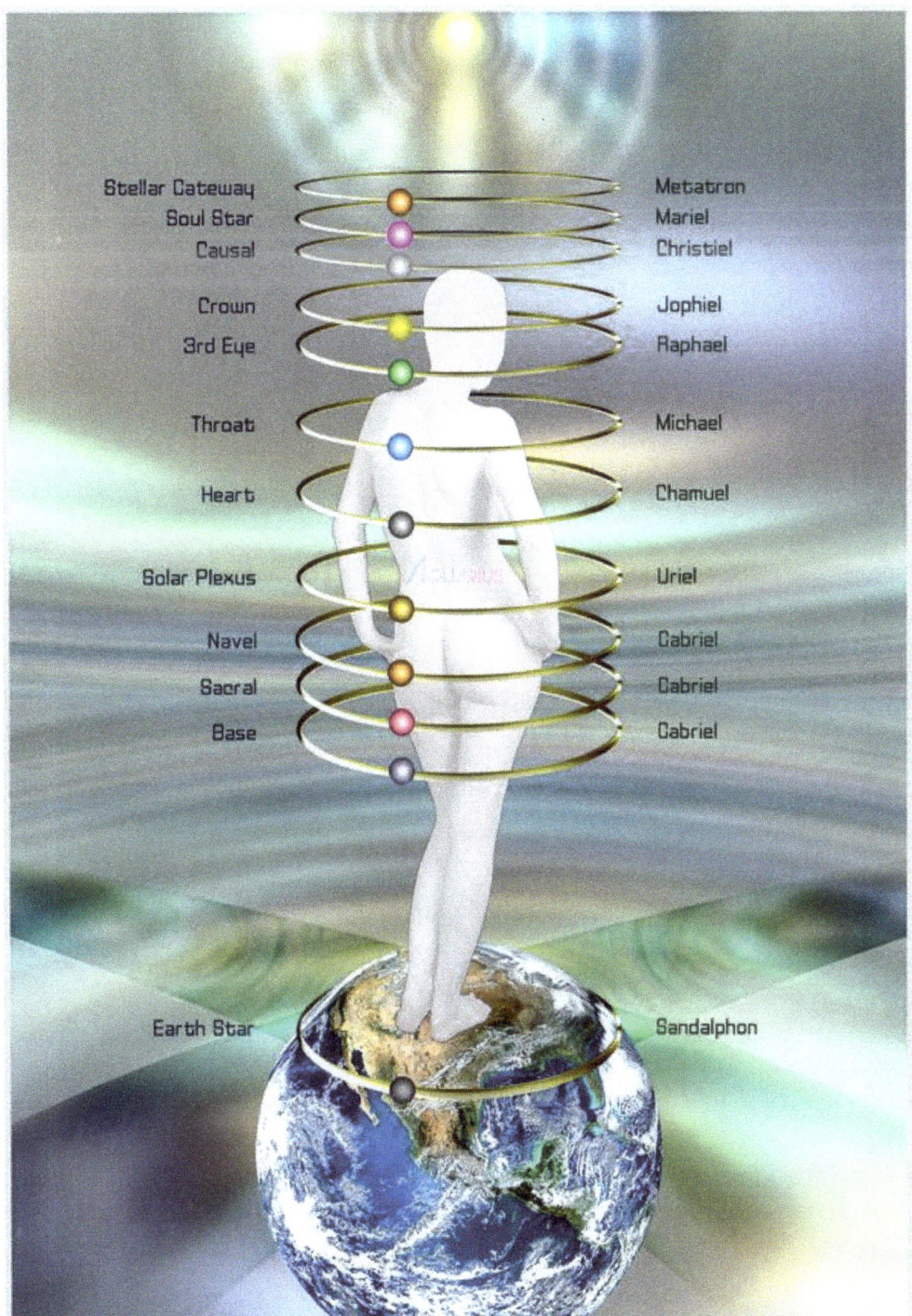

Here's another diagram of some of the main Chakra points, in the body and how they relate to special Angelic beings. It's incredible, there are angels for everything and we can call upon them anywhere and anytime for support, protection and healing. Same with asking God/Universe/Divine Creator, Jesus, Buddha, and other deity beings. In the higher realms everything is omnipresent where they can be present in multiple places anytime.

Cosmic Knowledge
Light Body
The Palm Chakras

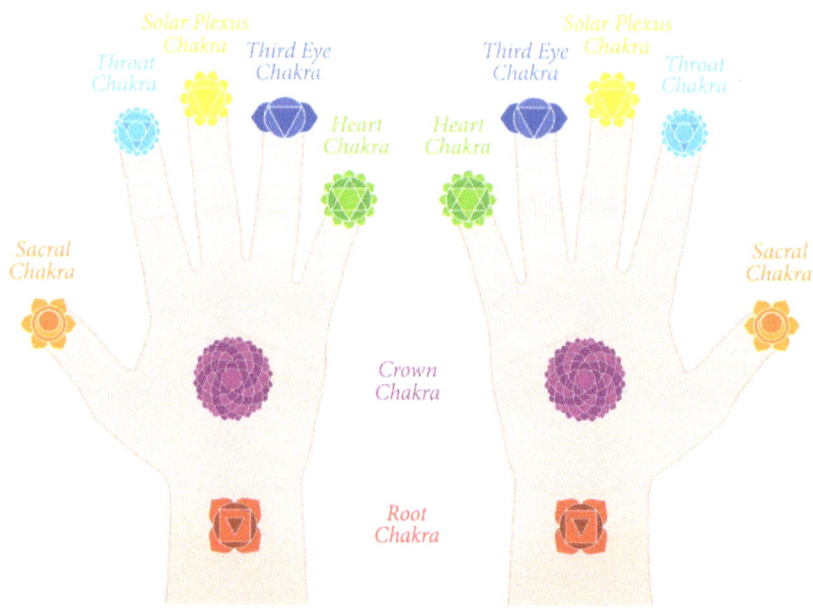

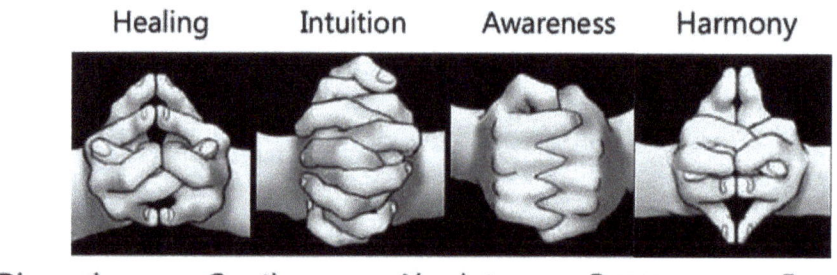

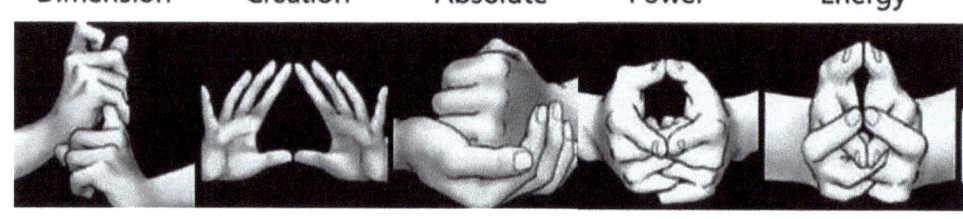

Just like our light bodies have intersecting energetic Chakra points, so do our hands and feet. We have many more smaller Chakra points all over our bodies. The hands have specialized ones that are like electrical circuits. When you place them in specific formations the Chakra points create a closed electrical circuit. Which then can provide extra energy to what you want to create by yourself or with another person. For example, when I do in person Higher Self readings, I put my thumb on the person's center palm Chakra. I then tap into their energetic soul sequence much more easily to gain information about them that I experience through my extrasensory abilities. It's like having wired internet connection instead of Wifi - they both work but the wired connection is much more energetically stable and faster.

Cosmic Knowledge
Light Body

As mentioned, the Auric/Torus field is made up of energetic layers. When it's full, healthy and vibrant you literally have a golden egg shaped space around your body that fully protects you from all negative parasitic beings & entities.

If yours is not in a good state, has holes or damage, you are susceptible to psychic attacks, loosh harvesting, possession, and negative attachments.

Cut all cords now and do the inner work to raise your vibrational energy and clear your field (see the practice section).

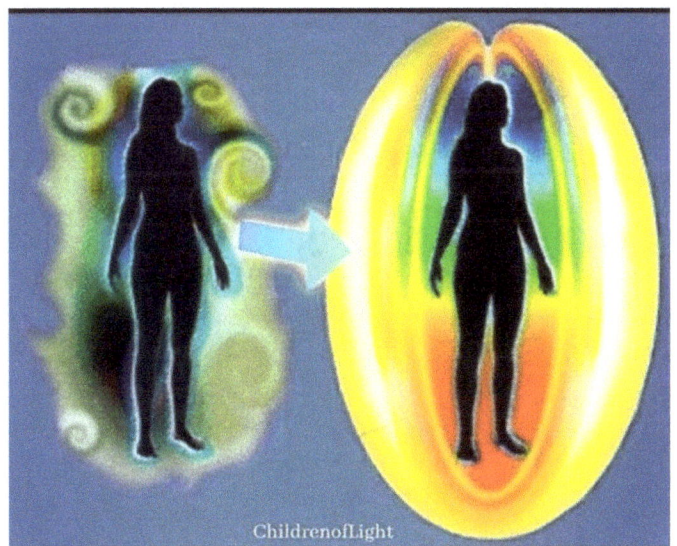

Ra: The Law of One is an exceptional series of books that makes so many things click and make sense. The image on the next page is from the Ra Materials which explains the human-etheric connection. The series was developed by three researchers in the 1980s that intentionally channeled information from an ancient collective consciousness, which is referred to as Ra. I highly recommend reading or listening to the book and videos on it. There's even free PDF versions of it online.

To sum it up, the moral lessons taught in the series are the main guiding principles of all the different types of beings in our universe - they know everything is divinely connected. Within this, there are three types of beings. Service to others, service to self and service to Creator = Benevolent, Malevolent, and Neutral, respectively. Even with differences such as these, all beings are all connected through oneness, Universal Oneness. That is the Law of One.

Cosmic Knowledge
Light Body

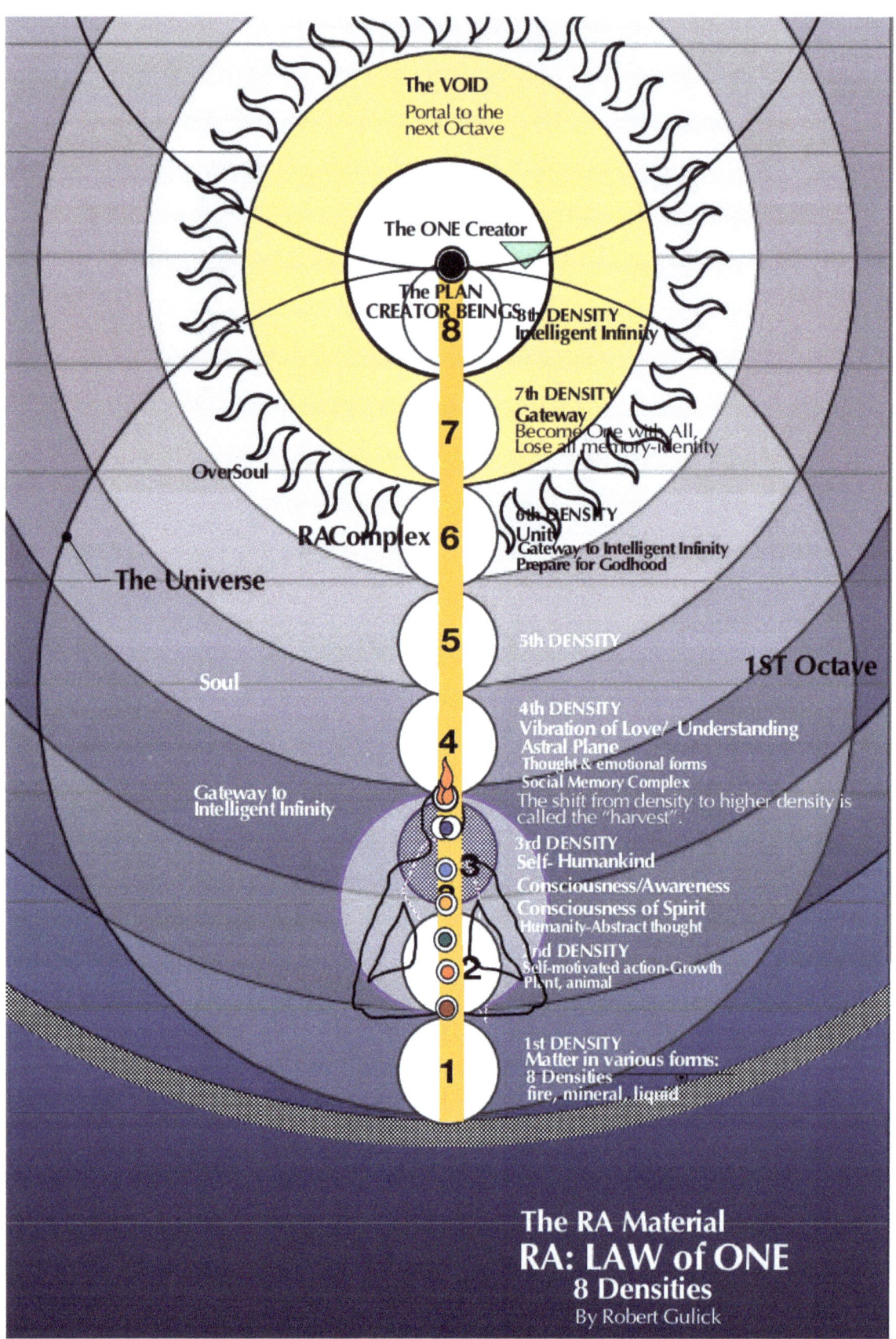

Cosmic Knowledge
Light Body

The Human light body, soul, spirit and Higher Self are layered like a mystical onion. We have the ability to intentionally go to any conscious level we choose, at will. Except we've forgotten how, how to do it, about our abilities and who we truly are. Why did we forget?

3D Earth "Death Trap: Reincarnation Cycle

Sounds a bit alarming and when you come to the full realization of it, it kind of is. Past life regression hypnotherapy specialists like Dolores Cannon and Michael Newton have regressed thousands of people and they all confirm this with unwavering accuracy. The oldest religion in the world among others also confirms the Samsara Reincarnation Cycle. So, what is it, how does it work and is it actually nefarious?

The Reincarnation cycle here is different than on other planets. Surface earth where us humans are, has been held in a specific 3rd dimensional vibration where there is extreme duality. For souls to incarnate here there are specific conditions and laws that must be adhered to such as having a physical 3D body with all its limitations, a baseline of 2D & 3D consciousness, soul contracts & missions, exit points (death), and before incarnation memory wipe. The memory wiping part makes us forget who we are, our powers, past lives, soul contracts, etc. The reasoning behind all of this is for a trinity of reasons - simply put "good, bad and neutral". There's duality and a further trinity meaning behind everything here. The bad or negative reason is for us to go through karma, experience pain and suffering, experience negative beings that feed off of our energy and can even trap us with karma. The benevolent or good side is that we can learn the most and obtain the most soul growth here than we can on other planets that are much easier and peaceful to incarnate on. And, the trinity or divine purpose is the universe / God consciousness experiencing life through unlimited fractals of itself. The Moon houses the reincarnation cycle also known as heaven which is located in the upper 4th dimension, called Nirvana. It's where souls go to rest, have a life review and create new soul contracts to reincarnate over and over again. Each planet has its own heaven but they differ from ours. Our is an AI simulation which traps the soul with a bright light right after death. If you don't want to go into the light you can turn the opposite direction and say "I want to go home". You will instantly travel to where your soul is most at home - wherever that may be in the cosmos.

It goes much deeper than this but this is to give you a basic explanation of it and that there are multiple purposes to why it's like this here. The good, bad and the higher purpose of it all.

Cosmic Knowledge
Types of Aliens

Cosmic Knowledge
Types of Aliens

Here's a short introductory list of just some of the beings that interact with humans and our planet. If one or more stick out to you, research them! There's many excellent pictures online, especially on Pinterest. You can also ask to connect with specific ones. There have been roughly 80 species cataloged publicly since 1920. Check out the Extraterrestrial Species Almanac book for more species, info & pictures.

1. Andromedans from Andromeda
2. Draco Reptilians from Earth & other systems
3. Zeta Greys from Zeta Reticuli
4. Pleiadians from Pleiades
5. Sirians from Sirius
6. Arcturians from Arcturius
7. Lyrans from Lyra
8. Venusians from Venus
9. Ganymedians from Ganymede (Jupiter Moon)
10. Mantis Beings
11. Blue, Red, Yellow, multi-coloured Avians
12. Insectoids from Earth & other planets
13. Agarthans / Anshar from Inner Earth
14. Martians from Mars
15. Essassani & Sassani Grey-Human Hybrids from Earth & nearby ships
16. Annunaki from Nibiru
17. Alpha Centaurians from Centaurus
18. Maldecians from Maldec (destroyed planet where asteroid belt is)
19. Gaseous Beings
20. RA & other collective consciousness beings
21. Koldashans
22. Klemers
23. Itipurians
24. Eridaneans
25. Cygnus Alphans
26. Cyclops
27. Clarons
28. Celestials
29. Ceitans
30. Cassiopeians from Cassiopea
31. Arians
32. Apunians
33. Altarians
34. Sagittarians from Sagittarius

Cosmic Knowledge
Types of Aliens

All in all there are over 300,000 different types of Aliens, Extraterrestrials, ETs, Star Beings, Isbe's, Interdimensionals, Humanoid Terrans, etc. in our Universe. Use whatever name suits your understanding and appreciate that our Universe is teeming with life! From the macro to the micro, life exists everywhere. We share the earth with many other types of Humanoid sentient beings too. Each one is just trying to live and get by in their own way, some eat plants or animals or humans while some regenerate through light or other forms of energy. Just because they do something that may go against us in some way, they're still just beings like us trying to live. They have their own drama, programming and problems too. Through this "Galactic Pilgrimage" we must remain open and don't judge them negatively for the way they are. But view them neutrally without reaction while standing in your power.

When I first heard about aliens on earth many years ago I thought "yeah right!" Laughing at how humorous it was. Especially when it comes to Reptilians. I thought it was hilarious how people believed in them and how stupid the whole thing sounded. I knew Aliens statistically had to exist based on the number of stars but here on earth, no way right? WRONG, I was so wrong. I was heavily programmed by TV, movies, news, school, church, and didn't even realize it. They've literally been hiding in plain sight all along and have been covered up so we could evolve to this point on our own.

David Wilcock, Billy Carson, Elizabeth April and the Farsight Institute are just a few of the many people that speak about the real truth. Aliens have been here all along and in fact much longer than humans have.

The history of all of everything would fill up many books. To sum it up, most things have been fabricated, even the Bible. It's correct for the most part but it's missing over 50 of the original books and gospels. The books have been strategically hidden to maintain control over the human population and for evolution, plus the divine purpose of us earning soul growth here.

As mentioned, Ra: The Law of One extensively explains the three main types of beings through a Q&A style of writing. I learned from a young age to feel a being's energetic sequence. Start practicing this wherever you go or people you see online. Practicing it will help you attune your abilities stronger & stronger.

1. **Benevolent / Service to others / Agreeable**
2. **Malevolent / Service to self / Disagreeable**
3. **Neutral / Service to the Divine Creator**

Cosmic Knowledge
Types of Aliens

Our universe is incomprehensibly massive. Every planet is or was inhabited already, has bases and entire civilizations living on but more than likely INSIDE of them. That's why we can't openly see them, except many bases and ships have been spotted as human camera technology has improved. There's even 3 million humans on Mars - many of which are slaves there too! Imagine what else and who else is out there.

They can't hide themselves anymore and know it's time for full contact. Bashar and others like Elizabeth April have mentioned there will be mass contact between 2026-2027. But we don't need to wait for them, we have already begun contact and can speed it up faster with this guidebook!

Cosmic Knowledge
Types of Aliens
Safeguards

It's important to know, there's way more benevolent Alien Star Beings out there than malevolent ones. However, we live in a very dualistic world with many negative parasitic entities running rampant. The negative ones often "make more noise" than the positive ones so that's why you may hear of them more often. They're fading out and are trying their last ditch efforts right now but they've already lost so don't focus on them, focus on the high vibes and high vibe beings!

How do you discern which has good or bad intentions? Negative ones will always try and trick you then make you do things that can harm you. The best way is to practice, here are some safeguards to help you out.

Ask them, are you God? 99% of the time a negative entity will say yes. God speaks in "I am, that I am" subtle ways and wouldn't say "yes, I am God". God and benevolent beings will radiate love. Anything that doesn't radiate love is there for you to learn discernment and practice transmutation. As mentioned, call upon your team prior to any contact to give you the highest vibrational light.

I've been doing this since I was a kid. When you feel/see/hear a being and they start engaging with you - feel their vibration - is it positive or negative? If positive keep engaging, if negative then tell it to leave now in a strong powerful voice (not angry just firm) or you can transmute that entity. To transmute them, ask your angels & guides to help you. Fill your bodies with crystalline white light and shoot it out of your 3rd eye or heart Chakra at them. They will either run away or burst back into Source energy. We are masters of transmutation and don't even realize it fully yet.

Another two safeguards are to surround yourself with golden bright crystalline energy and to connect into your 5D Higher Self. See the practice area for more info and always, do your own research and find what works for you.

You will be guarded with love, always. Remember, you are DOUBLE if not more powerful than any low vibratory entity and they are terrified of you and all humans waking up to our true power. We could wipe them all out easily if we all collectively and intentionally transmuted all lower vibrational energy into crystalline high vibrational energy. Humans are prophesied to obliterate lower energies from this universe. We have a massive task at hand and are completely capable of it! If you want to learn more about the Human Prophecy check out Elizabeth April's video on it for free on YouTube and her website.

By reading this, doing the inner work and outer work, you are helping yourself and all of humanity progress forward. We got this!

Cosmic Knowledge
Psychic Abilities

All of humanity is waking up and evolving right now. As the vibration rises up more and more people awaken. They start to become in tune with themselves and the universe.

All races of beings go through this process - the Ascension process. Where their consciousness rises up into higher states. They had other beings helping them through their ascension and now it's their time to help us. One day, we will help other beings through their Ascension and so on. There are millions of beings that are studying, experimenting on, and watching us right now. They are also training on their side to be able to communicate with us. As you develop your interdimensional communication skills you are also helping them to make the Galactic Pilgrimage go more smoothly.

Cosmic Knowledge
Psychic Abilities

1. **Astral projection or mental projection –** The ability to voluntarily project an astral body or mental body, being associated with the out-of-body experience, in which one's consciousness is felt to temporarily separate from the physical body.
2. **Atmokinesis –** The ability to control the weather such as calling rainfall or storms.
3. **Portal Manipulation** - creating, closing, neutralizing, and/or manipulating portals.
4. **Automatic writing –** The ability to draw or write without conscious intent.
5. **Bilocation/ Mind Travel —** The ability to be present in two different places at the same time.
6. **Energy medicine –** The ability to heal with one's own empathic, etheric, astral, mental or spiritual energy.
7. **Ergokinesis -** The ability to influence the movement of energy, such as electricity, without direct interaction.
8. **Levitation or transvection –** The ability to float or fly by mystical means.
9. **Materialization —** The creation of objects and materials or the appearance of matter from unknown sources (easy and fun to do in the astral realm).
10. **Mediumship or channeling –** The ability to communicate with spirits.
11. **Petrification —** The power to turn a living being to stone by looking them in the eye.
12. **Prophecy (also prediction, premonition, or prognostication) —** the ability to foretell events, without using induction or deduction from known facts.
13. **Psychic surgery –** The ability to remove disease or disorder within or over the body tissue via an "energetic" incision that heals immediately afterwards.
14. **Psychokinesis or telekinesis –** The ability to influence a physical system without physical interaction, typically manifesting as being able to exert force, control objects and move matter with one's mind.
15. **Pyrokinesis –** The ability to control flames, fire, or heat using one's mind.
16. **Iddhi –** Psychic abilities gained through Buddhist meditation.
17. **Shapeshifting or transformation —** The ability to physically transform the user's body into anything (also easy and fun to do in the astral realm).
18. **Thoughtography -** The ability to impress an image by 'burning' it on a surface using one's own mind only.

Psychic Abilities

19. Xenoglossy — The ability of a person to suddenly learn to write and speak a foreign language without any natural means such as studying or research, but that is often rather bestowed by divine agents.

20. **Witnessing -** The gift of being visited by high profile spiritual beings such as Mary, Jesus or Fudosama (Acala) from Buddhist Traditions.

21. **Inedia -** The ability to survive without eating or drinking, multiple cases have resulted in starvation or dehydration. (Don't try this! You have a 3D body & it needs real food.)

(Wikipedia, 2023)

22. Extrasensory Perception & Tools

Extrasensory perception, or sixth sense, is an ability in itself as well as comprising a set of abilities. These are best viewed as an extension of our physical abilities.

- **Clairvoyance —** The ability to see things and events that are happening far away, and locate objects, places, people, using a sixth sense.
- **Divination –** The ability to gain insight into a situation using occult lists. (Tarot cards, pendulum, tea leaves, Runes, flame or water scrying, palmistry, face & eye reading).
- **Dowsing –** The ability to locate water, sometimes using a tool called a dowsing rod.
- **Dream telepathy -** The ability to telepathically communicate with another person through dreams.
- **Dermo-optical perception -** The ability to perceive unusual sensory stimuli through one's own skin.
- **Psychometry or psychoscopy –** The ability to obtain information about a person or an object by touch.
- **Precognition (including psychic premonitions) –** The ability to perceive or gain knowledge about future events, without using induction or deduction from known facts.
- **Remote viewing, telesthesia or remote sensing –** The ability to see a distant or unseen target using extrasensory perception.
- **Claircognizant Retrocognition or postcognition –** The ability to supernaturally perceive past events.
- **Telepathy –** The ability to transmit or receive thoughts supernaturally.

(Wikipedia, 2023)

Attunement

There are even more psychic abilities that extend through our physical bodies and are unique based on our specializations & skills. It makes us all unique. Write out what abilities you have and how you use them. Keep a journal of how they change and expand through your attunement and contact process.

To have the best foundation for communication with interdimensional alien beings, here are the main layers humans need to attune to higher frequencies to create the ideal state for connecting with Star Beings.

Physical, Emotional, Mental, Energetic, Spiritual, Etheric, Quantum, & Cosmic.

Attunement

Attunement of Each Layer

1. **Physical:** cleanse out heavy metals, toxins and parasites. Eat clean with lots of fresh organic, fruits, veggies herbs, & meats. Little to no processed foods*
2. **Emotional:** Clear your karma, gain healthy coping & self soothing skills, learn emotional intelligence, do somatic healing and move your fascia which often stores your emotions.
3. **Mental:** Heal your trauma, work on your Vagus nerve, use cognitive behavioral therapy (CBT) and positive affirmations for 21 days, and shift old paradigms. Calming and controlling rampant monkey brain.
4. **Energetic:** become energetically aware, balance divine feminine and masculine energies, cleanse and strengthen your energetic bodies. Smudge & cut chords!
5. **Spiritual:** Spiritual healing with the creator and belief systems, dark night of the soul / ego death.
6. **Etheric:** 4D shadow work, uncovering lies and truths, decrement, 5D+ Consciousness Activations, practice.
7. **Quantum:** Upper 4D, 5D and beyond quantum realms, learn quantum jumping & increase your awareness of dimensions & beings.
8. **Cosmic:** Cosmic Collective Consciousness connection & connection to the Divine / God / Creator through love, forgiveness, peace, enlightenment, appreciation & joy. Honoring all life - especially all of the plants and animals we eat, they're all conscious too!

Attunement

Vibrational attunement is essential to ascension, DNA & neurological pathway expansion to be able to access higher dimensional frequencies for communication with other dimensional beings. Attunement of the physical body is essential as it can tether us into 3D and make it much more dense and difficult to raise our vibration for ET contact. High vibrational beings that came to me at the end of 2019 explained some these keys things must be done and I learned about some of these on my journey as well:

More Attunement Methods

- Look at, draw out, and study sacred geometry each day
- Listen to Solfeggio Frequencies and/or Binaural Beats
- Dr. Joe Dispenza's brain & heart coherence meditations
- Kundalini meditations to activate the spinal fluid upward into the pineal gland
- Eating *living & energized/fresh* natural foods that nourish your cells - it may surprise you but fruit, some veggies and meat are all important
- Chakra clearing and activation
- Movement, walking, hiking, dancing, yoga, swimming
- Tree hugging, connecting to nature and earthing
- Sunrise or sunset gazing - taking in solar energy
- Get lots of sunlight - the more the better! 90% of people are deficient in vitamin D which is essential for hundreds of processes in the body
- Float with sensory deprivation
- Do anything that brings joy, love, peace and enlightenment
- Sway method of connecting into your body and asking questions. Typically, your body will sway forward for yes and backward for no.
- Raise your vibration
- Clear & heal trauma from the body, mind & soul
- Cleanse the body of toxins, parasites & heavy metals
- Clear the mind of negative thoughts & patterns
- Release all energies, patterns and habits not serving our highest purpose
- Create and/or become involved with benevolent groups
- Give up meat, eggs, fish and dairy to help with the physical cleansing process (temporary - for 2-3 months. Consult with a trained professional)
- Soul fragmentation repair (Akashic Records, Access Bars & Reiki can help!)
- Gain a beautiful understanding and deeper respect for animals and plants that are soul contracted to eat. They all have spirit within them. Acknowledge & honor them.
- Listen to what my body needs, seek out craving charts of what your body is really asking for.

Attunement

Reprogramming the Reticular Activating System

Rewire your brain for gratitude, love , prosperity, joy, 5D consciousness, or whatever you desire. This begins with rewiring your reticulated activating system. The reticular activating system is the brain's filtering system. The eyes see millions of pixels but the brain can only process a fraction of them without getting overloaded (which often happens - sensory overload). Our brain fills in the rest of the space with our imagination and subconscious mind. This system is programmed by our neurological pathways which are programmed from age 0 to 8 years, major life events, stressful or painful or happy events, and by our thoughts and emotional responses. We're like these extremely complex computer systems that have the ability to rewire our on motherboard.

See the Gratitude practice exercise for full details & how to do it. Also listen to Dr. Joe Dispenza, Brian Scott, and Louise Hay for reprogramming your RAS.

Emotional & Chemical Regulation

Dr. Joe Dispenza speaks about the chemical response that happens within the body when a person is in a state of anger or distress. When an emotional response occurs, the body will release stress hormone chemicals like cortisol. That often gives an intense boost of sensations that lasts for 30 to 90 seconds. If a person is still angry after 90 seconds, they're choosing to perpetuate that anger and the body will often give them "another hit" of cortisol. There's actually cortisol addictions where a person can be addicted to drama because of the cortisol release. Detoxing from natural body chemicals and hormones is very helpful in the attunement process. Along with being consciously aware of your triggers and to learn how to observe non-reactively. When you can master this and what's also referred to in Buddhist "rampant monkey brain". When communicating and interfacing with Aliens or any type of spirit or being - you must have calm emotions and a calm mind. Meditation is so helpful and needed for all humans to practice and take part in.

Soul Retrieval

As mentioned, our souls can become fractured or split by traumatic events in our lives, from past lives or toxic ways of thinking. Here's how to start to claim all parts of yourself back: Say out loud: "I call all parts of my soul back now". Akashic Records, Reiki, Access Bars/Body Talk can also help too.

Attunement
Soul Journey to Know Thyself

These are things to look into to get to know yourself, heal, clear, cleanse, bring power, protection and guidance to. If you have an existing belief / programming of something being negative that's how it can affect you. Realizing those unconscious beliefs and eliminating /changing them is key for moving forward 🔑 We are extremely powerful beings and can transfer energy into and out of things. Be wise with your words, thoughts and actions.

Astrology
Life Number
Soul Missions
Past Lives
Soul Level
Crystals

Living Your Passion
Spirit Guides
Guardian Angels
Higher Self
Soul Origin
Intentional Living

Attunement
Soul Journey to Know Thyself

<u>Astrology:</u> The study of a person's planetary alignment at the exact moment they were born. This is like the textbook example of your strengths and weaknesses, tendencies, preferences, energy flow, compatibility and many more things. It's important to note Astrology is different from horoscopes that only look at one of the signs - The Sun Sign. In fact, we have a sign for every planet in the solar system, plus a midheaven, rising, and all sorts of different house signs that correspond with parts of our lives. It's complicated yes, but important to recognize this is not the end all be all to who you are - life, parents, friends, lovers, experiences shape us too. Visit Astro-Charts.com to find out your Astrological chart for free.

<u>Life Number:</u> A person's Life number is from 1 to 9 and indicates your natural strengths, weaknesses and life purpose. You add up your full birth day, year, month and keep adding the numbers until you're at a single digit. For example, my birthday is 01-10-1987 = 1+1+1+9+8+7= 27 = 2+7 = 9. The life number 9 is associated with completion, transformation, and balance and is believed to have a powerful influence on human destiny and the universe as a whole. There's a lot more to it, check out <u>numerology.com</u> for all the info.

<u>Soul Missions:</u> Along with soul contracts, we have soul missions to complete to varying degrees. Some people are here just to generally raise the vibration, while some have more specific missions like to write books about humans making contact with Aliens. No matter what it is, they're all individually and collectively important. Elizabeth April's book "You're Not Dying, You're Just Waking Up" goes through the types of soul missions here.

<u>Past Lives & Ancestral Lines:</u> Gaining insight into your past life times and your ancestral DNA lines can be extremely helpful to know what type and how much karmic debt you have, curses, stuck trauma, Cosmic keys, gifts - plus, how to clear and/or hone them.

<u>Soul Level:</u> In Michael Newton's book "Journey of Souls" it goes through the different soul levels and breaks them into newer, middle, older and ancient souls. Most people often think they're an old soul when they're actually much newer or even mid-leveled. It's key to find out where you're at to give you a clearer picture of how much soul work you have ahead of yourself.

<u>Crystals:</u> Crystals can help heal, bring greater awareness and activations. We each have stones that will be of benefit more to us than others. Find which ones can help you along your journey.

Attunement
Soul Journey to Know Thyself

<u>Living Your Passion:</u> Being in full alignment to your passions is essential to activating your gifts and pursuing your soul missions. Are you doing what you're most passionate about? If not, here is your sign to start it now!

<u>Spirit Guides & Guardian Angels:</u> Because this incarnation is so challenging we all have multiple helpers in the etheric realms. We each have one or more guardian angels and a team of Spirit Guides. They each can vary greatly from person to person but often they have been with us for multiple incarnations and are here to help us - but sometimes they can also work to our detriment. You can "fire" a spirit guide if they're not helping you.

<u>Higher Self:</u> Your Higher Self is at least two or more incarnation soul levels above where you're currently at. So, in 3D your Higher Self will be your 4-5D self. If you're 5D activated your Higher Self could be in 6-7D or even higher. Every soul is unique and is here for a plethora of reasons.

<u>Soul Origin:</u> By knowing your soul origin you can understand deeper meanings to how you react to things here on earth. Majority of Starseeds are appalled by human behavior because more than likely on their home planet was in service to others and very peaceful. I often feel weird doing human everyday things, I forgot that I'm used to using telekinesis to put things away or get things😂.

<u>Intentional Living:</u> This means you're in control of your life and are not letting outside things influence your thoughts, emotions, decisions, choices, eating living foods, etc. Easier said than done, but it's possible to do this through training and attunement.

You may be wondering, how? Here are the ways
you can find out specific information about you:

- Hypnotherapy / past life regression / QHHT
- Akashic Records reading
- Psychic reading   ← **Slightly More Accurate**
- Body Talk / Access Bars

- Channeling (you or someone else)
- Remote viewing
- Astral Travel   ← **Slightly Less Accurate**
- Deep meditation
- Asking your guides & angels

Attunement
Soul Journey to Know Thyself

Multi-Dimensional Self

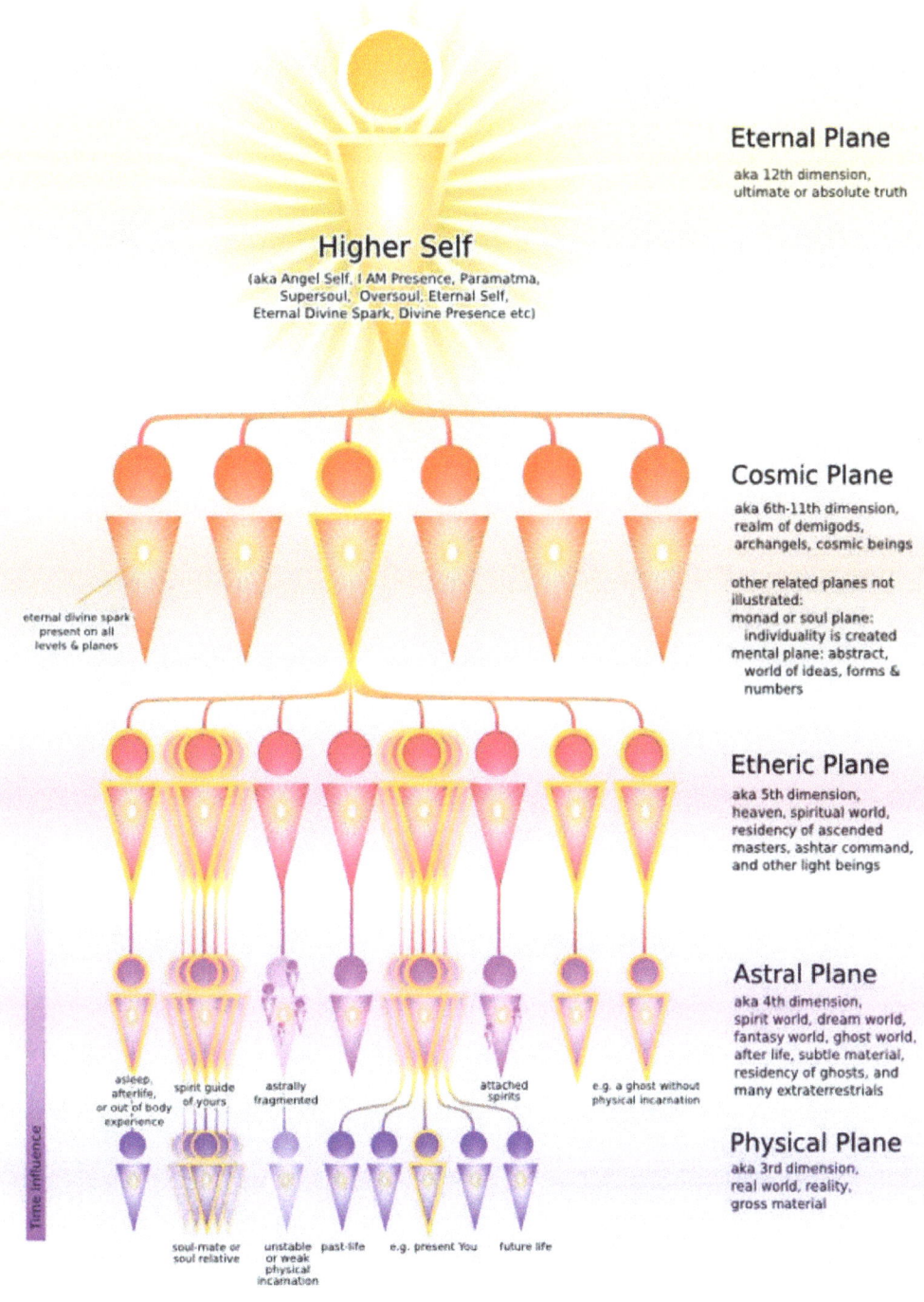

As mentioned, your Higher Self is at least two or more ascension levels above you and in reality we have multiple Higher Selves and is ultimately like your God consciousness self. This diagram is absolutely fascinating and gives a great overview of all the parts that make up your soul - we are so beautifully complex. An important part to note is in the Astral Plane there can be soul fragmentation which can cause many issues especially with our identity. You can reclaim it though!

Ways of Communication

Humans are incredibly powerful beings. We share DNA with many different types of light and shadow beings (approx. 22-24 types). We have 12 strands of DNA but typically only 2-3 are consciously activated.

As we ascend into higher dimensions our DNA will expand and our neurological pathways in our brain and throughout our body. We will all become more psychic, have the ability to levitate, move things with our mind and see future events. As you can see on the previous pages, there are many different types of energetic abilities, ways to utilize and hone them. It's like exercising your muscles at the gym, you need to practice consistently to build on them and get toned. Our mind is the same way.

Now is the time to figure out what your special gifts are and work on honing them. This is why you came here. Enjoy the over 30 different ways of communication on the next page!

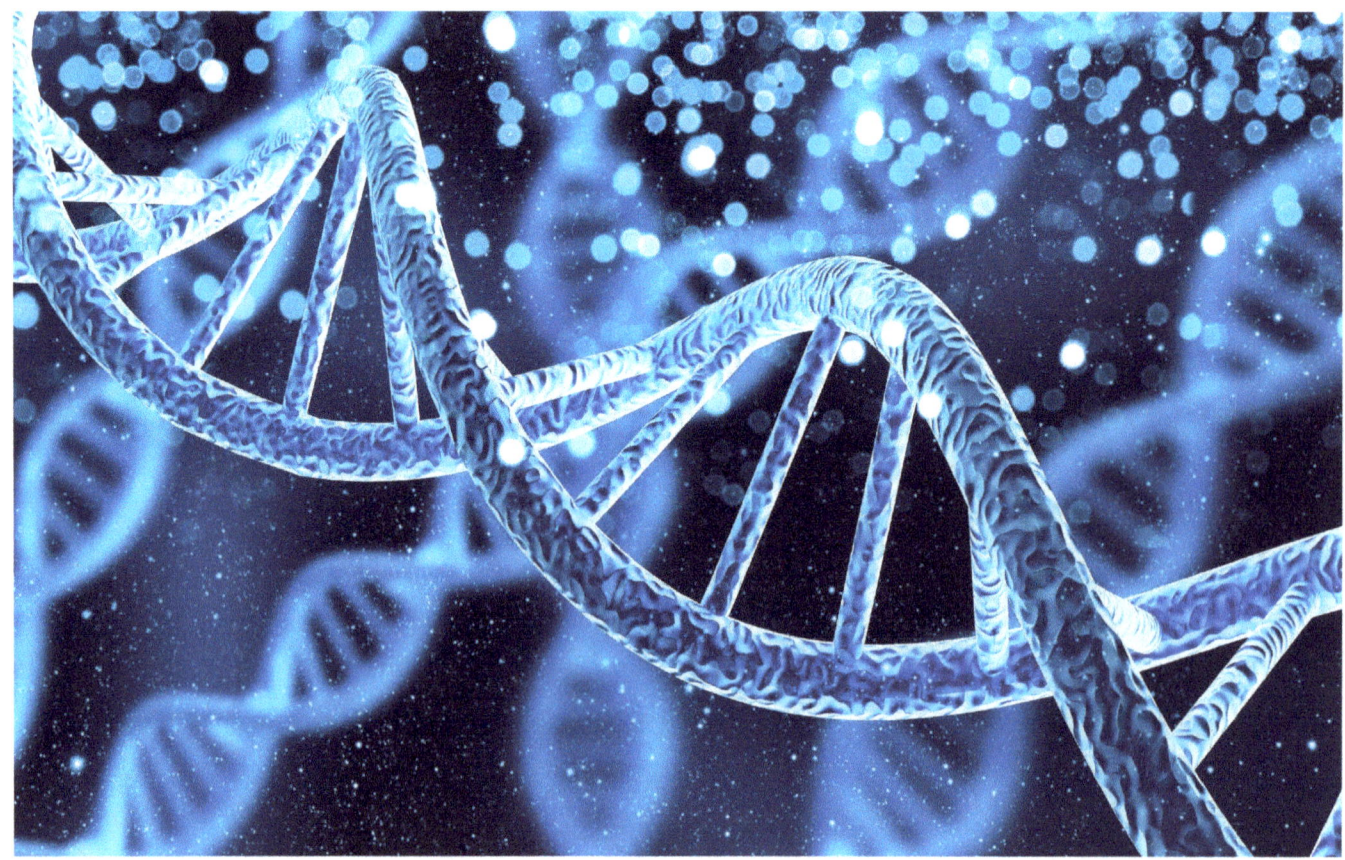

Ways of Communication

1. Interfacing
2. Telepathy
3. Clairvoyance
4. Clairaudient
5. Claircognizance
6. Clairsentience
7. Clairempathy
8. Clairsalient
9. Clairtangency
10. Clairintellect
11. Clairgustance
12. Ujjayi Breathing Techniques
13. Astral Travel / Projection
14. Lucid Dreaming
15. Remote Viewing
16. CE1, CE2, CE3, CE4, CE5
17. Merkabah Light Body
18. Channeling & Automatic writing
19. Downloading from the fields
20. Hypnotherapy
21. Transcendental Meditation
22. Akashic Records
23. Psychedelics
24. Synchronicities
25. Messages from Other People
26. Messages from Animals & Plants
27. Dreams, Deja Vu & Day Dreams
28. OBE
29. NDE
30. Soul Contracts

Ways of Communication

There are even more ways to make contact than this list but it shows there are many different types of ways we can interdimensional make contact, receive and send information. More often than not, you're already doing things to communicate with beings and that they too are already communicating with you. You may or may not even know, yet.

How is this all possible? As mentioned in the dimensional graphs, we're existing on many dimensions and densities within each dimension. So are these beings. It sounds crazy from a 3rd dimensional science and medical perspective. That's because anything 3D completely negates the higher dimensions. So, in saying this people only in 3D and lower consciousness cannot begin to comprehend higher dimensions. All the studies, literature, courses, etc are all trapped in the 3rd dimension conscious awareness. All current standardized systems on earth are trapped and locked into 3D - financial, educational, medical, travel, pharmaceutical, mechanical, physics, communication, etc.

It is nearly impossible for a person to use 3D science to fully understand ET beings, etheric energy, quantum science, etc because they go beyond the 3rd dimension. They're not wrong but just making assumptions within one confined physical dimension. There's a veil that exists between the dimensions. By using your psychic abilities / Clairs you can pierce through the veil into the 4th & 5th+ dimension or 2nd density.

There's a considerable amount of skepticism around all of this plus the religious aspect of it often brings fear into the mix. First, there's nothing to fear by using your God given gifts. Second, the Bible was heavily edited so humanity wouldn't be able to have the full picture. Now we know the full picture and know that we are way more powerful than anything negatively oriented. Third, don't give away your power, stay out of fear and in your heart center.

The truth about the Bible is that it's right, it's correct BUT it's missing OVER 50 BOOKS!!! They were strategically removed by King James to keep humanity from the real truth of our origins, connections to Aliens, they even removed reincarnation! Then had the audacity to change parts of the Bible basically saying "you only have one life here be good or else you're going to hell". I encourage you to read the Apocrypha , the Book of Enoch, Thomas, Mary, Joseph, the Dead Sea Scrolls, Epic of Gilgamesh and every Billy Carson video out there to get that whole picture - then make up your mind.

Ways of Communication

1. Interfacing: when two or more beings are communicating with telepathy, with Clairs or another extrasensory ability.

2. Telepathy: this is telepathically communicating between two or more beings. Telepathy is not reading someone's mind but more so being on the same frequency for non-verbal completely etheric communication. This can be achieved when your vibrational frequency is in a heightened state such as Gamma or Alpha brain waves with an open and loving heart and pineal gland. In the next pages I will discuss these in more detail along with the rest of the ways of communication and how to get into those states.

Key: speak in a commanding voice, visualize what you're trying to communicate in your mind then imagine that image going out, feel it, the vibration of it. Command it.

The image on the next page is of the pineal gland being activated through meditation. It is exactly like a radio tower beaming out signals and receiving them back. Often times during meditation you may feel a whirling of energy that moves your body in a circle. As you can see in this image starting at the base of his neck it shows the twisting energy chords that connect through the Chakras and out through the crown.

KEY 🔑 most of the words humans speak are unfortunately energetically meaningless. They are empty. There's a key difference between empty words and words that have passion, higher vibration and meaning. It's especially noticeable when manifesting and is a reason many people fail to manifest what they desire because what they speak doesn't have enough of the soul's vibrational essence in it. So, how do you have more purpose, passion and soul essence in your words? With energy channeling. Interestingly enough, I first learned energy channeling through opera - your power center for vocals is in your solar plexus Chakra but in order to properly activate your voice, you must ground your energy downward into the ground. Once you're grounded, you pull energy up from the earth by inhaling in deeply, bring it into your feet, through your legs up through your pelvis, abdomen, chest, throat and exhale it out through the top of your head. Connect that energy to Source / God ? Divine Creator. Practice this each day.

Ways of Communication

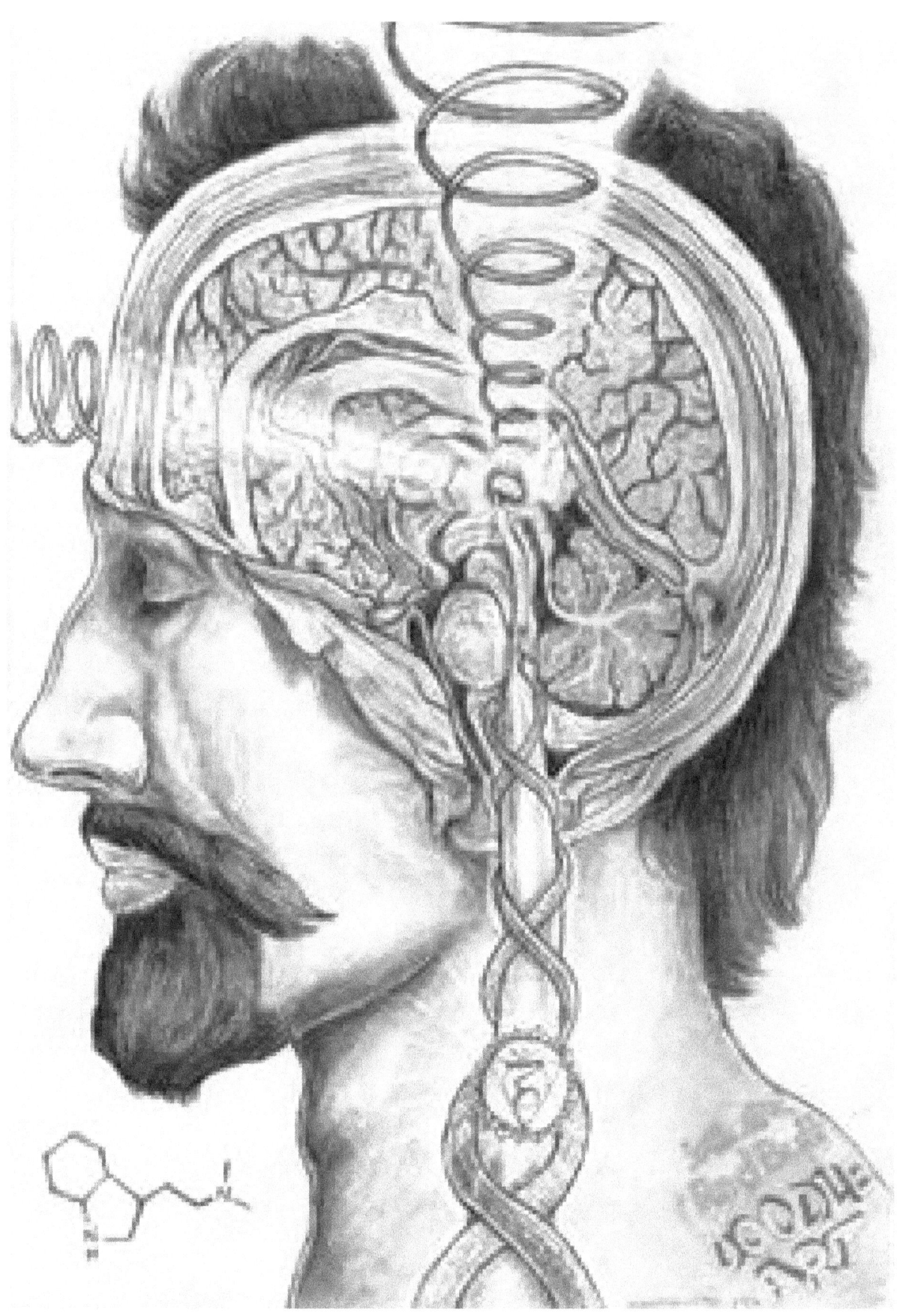

Ways of Communication

Each of our Clairs are ways beings, souls, spirits, Aliens, Star Beings, plants and animals can communicate with us. Knowing how to interpret, put out, and discern are very important. Here's a diagram of how to command your physical human vessel to communicate.

YOUR VOICE COMMANDS YOUR MIND, BODY AND SPIRIT

Learn the true meaning of each word, the root and original intention. Find the cousins to each word, say it, feel it, which one will move you forward in your own life?

I can't	• Will literally stop growth
I won't	• Will literally put a block in your way
	• Can mont is a command to self
It's hard =	• Will literally stop you from achieving anything in your life
I don't believe	• Is a taught behavior that is a conditional to hold a person back
I'm a skeptic	• Stops a person from learning
I don't like it	• Stops a person from gaining intellect (IQ)

ENERGY + VIBRATION = MATTER

THOUGHT IS ENERGY
SEEING IS ENERGY
TALKING IS VIBRATION
SPEAKING IS VIBRATION

Try	• Try and you will do it over and over never get to the end.
Trying	• Puts a block in your way
	• Try is a command to self
I can try =	• Try and trying is a taught behavior that is a condition to hold a person back
I'm trying	• It has very little or not results
I will try	• It is like running a race with no end
	• It is never ending
I will attempt	• It is repetitious

THOUGHTS + VOICE = REALITY
Help the self by Walking the Absolute Truth of your own life. Meditate and Pray...Keep thoughts, actions & words positive... Be self empowered and use the tools presented in a good way.

I can	• Literally promotes growth
I am	• Can is a command to self
I believe =	• Allows your wants and needs and desires to come true
It is done	• is a behavior of using good words
I can do it	• It is unconditional and moves a person forward in life
I can do anything	• When you know inside you can do it, your body needs to hear it
	• Your body reacts to key words

Adapted from a slide by Barbara M. Moreau, Angel who dances on the Clouds and Frank J. Austin, Manyhorses (Teacher)

Ways of Communication

We have the ability to communicate with anything and everything, especially living beings like trees. They are a joy to connect & communicate with. Plus, excellent beings to start your telepathic practice with. Try these!

■ The energy exchange in befriending a tree can be felt in cycles especially in the third, sixth, ninth and so on

■ Your aura is an electromagnetic field that blends with all matter. Visualize a bright white light around your body and the tree

■ Your first option is to visualize that your energy is coming out from the top of your head (as a bright white light) that passes on to the top of the tree

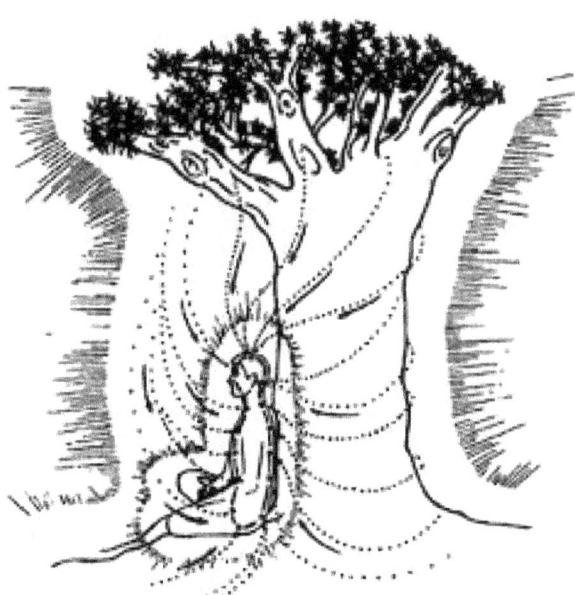

■ Simply place your back to the tree as you meditate or do

Ways of Communication

3-11. The Clairs / Sixth Senses / Extra-sensory Abilities

3. Clairvoyance (clear seeing)
4. Clairaudience (clear hearing)
5. Clairsentience (clear feeling)
6. Claircognizance (clear knowing)
7. Clairempathy (clear emotion)
8. Clairtangency (clear touching)
9. Clairalience (clear smelling)
10. Clairgustance (clear tasting)
11. Clairintellect (clear thinking)

The Clairs is a short form for many different types of energetic abilities or sixth senses or extrasensory abilities. We all have these abilities within us, some will come more easily than others as everyone is unique and different. These are extensions of our physical abilities (5 senses) into the etheric 4D, 5D and above realms. We all have them and have the ability to tap into them.

Clairvoyance
(clear seeing)

Clairaudience
(clear hearing)

Claircognizance
(clear knowing)

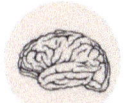
Clairintellect
(clear thinking)

Clairempathy
(clear emotion)

Clairsentience
(clear physical feeling)

Clairtangency
(clear touching)

Clairsalience
(clear smelling)

Clairgustance
(clear tasting)

reikilifestyle.com

Ways of Communication

The Clairs

3. Clairvoyance: Clear Seeing - seeing images in your mind (3rd eye pineal gland) of past, present or future events.

4. Clairaudient: Clear Hearing - is hearing something in the past, present or future. This can often be misdiagnosed as schizophrenia because the 3D medical system negates 4D, 5D and above science. It is very real and the majority of humans have this ability naturally but are trained to ignore it - much like the other Clairs.

5. Clairsentience: Clear Feeling - is a feeling of knowing something about someone or thing. The heart and gut brains (Vagus Nerve) play a key role in this as our feeling abilities extend outward through them. This is also known as a gut feeling, unction, Spidey sense, and intuition.

6. Claircognizance: Clear Thinking - also known as Precognition, when you cognitively know something will happen before it does. Another common name is Deja Vu meaning already seen.

7. Clairempathy: Clear Emotion - All Empaths have this, you clearly feel other people's or being's emotions. Telepathy uses empathy as a communication method as to be "on the same wavelength".

8. Clairtangency: Clear Touching - also known as Psychometry is the ability to touch something and get information from that object. Everything is made up of energy - events, people, things can leave energetic imprints, especially when something traumatic happens. Clairtangency reads the energy imprints.

9. Clairalience: Clear Smelling - the sense of smell can jog a memory or event from the past, present or future. Also be a signal of something happening the person is nowhere near.

Ways of Communication

10. Clairgustance: Clear tasting - Many chefs have this, the ability to taste something without it being made and then creating it. Or being able to taste something someone else is experiencing.

11. Clairintellect: Clear Intellect - I strongly feel this Clair is the ability to directly channel your Higher Self and/or the collective consciousness. You know when your mind is so sharp and you already know things before they happen, you're in tune with your reality.

12. Ujjayi Breathing: also referred to as pranayama is a specific way of breathing that activates the pineal gland which can allow for relaxation, healing, ability to send & receive data, induce astral projection, Kundalini activation and even Merkabah activation. See the simplified Ujjayi Breathing exercise in the practice section.

13. Astral Projection Techniques: The act of getting into a deep meditative state where the physical body completely relaxes then purposely moving the astral body out of the physical body. There are various techniques to get into astral projection, you have to find what works for you. There are multiple examples in the practice section.

Ways of Communication

14. Lucid Dreaming: Become Conscious in Dreams and the ability to control what you do in dream state. This is similar to Astral Travel and is another

15. Remote Viewing: it is a technique that uses the clairvoyant abilities in a specific sequence to view events, people, and things. With remote viewing you can view the past, present and future. This has been heavily studied for decades by individuals and government officials, particularly in the FBI and CIA. You can view the FBI Vault online for the Remote Viewing protocols under Project Stargate and Extrasensory Perception.

The Farsight Institute offers a free remote viewing course and Dr. Steven Greer has a DVD course. In the practice section you'll find a basic overview of how to remote view subjects.

16. Close Encounters (CE5's) Dr. Steven Greer created specific protocols to contact benevolent Star Beings through his CE5 app using a bi-location method. This is great to do by yourself or in a group of people. The app shows other CE5 people in your local area that you can message to connect with. It's a great place to meet like minded, awakened people who share the same goals.

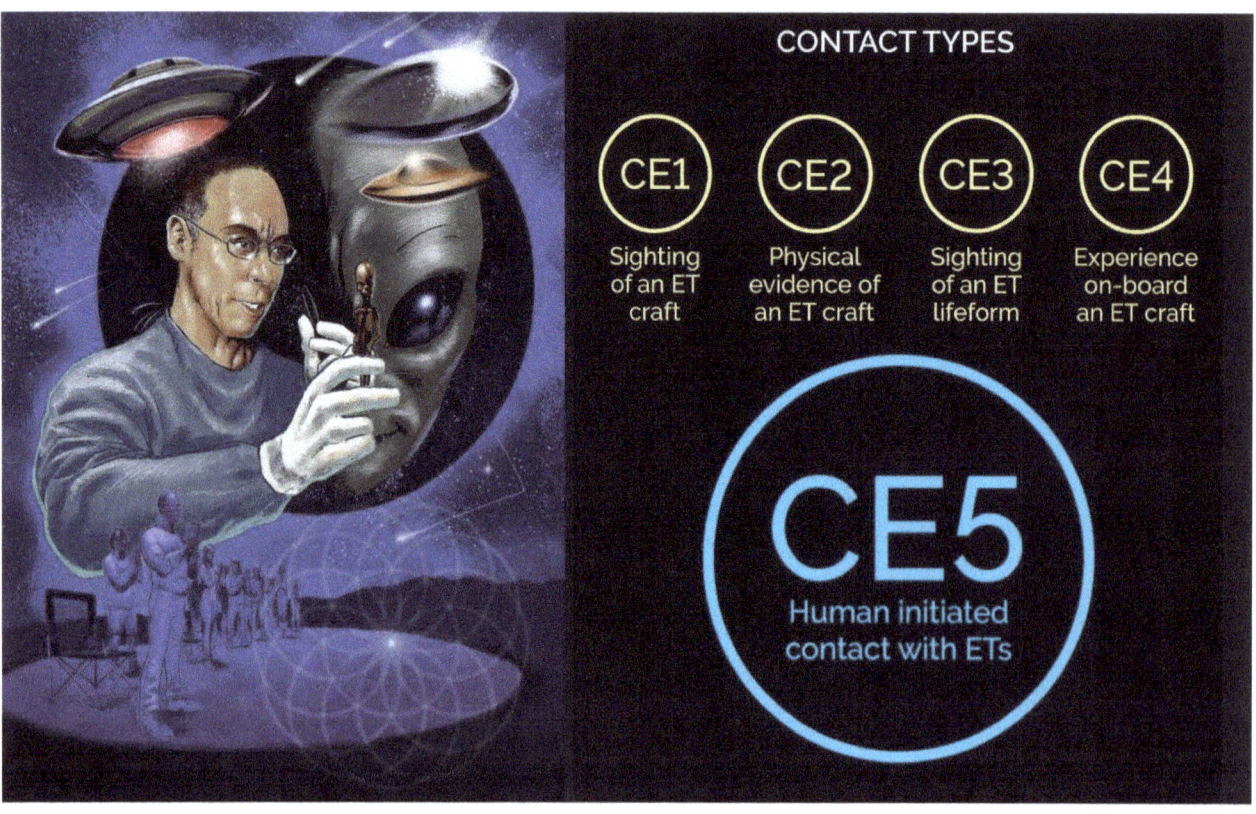

Ways of Communication

17. Merkabah Light Body: it symbolizes the body's "chariot" which is a full light activated way to travel through space time. This differs from Astral Travel as that is the astral body traveling whereas this is all layers of the light body activation to allow for further and more accurate distance traveling. This is the typical way for other light beings to travel - especially Plaeidians. In the practice area I speak about this more and give resources on how to activate yours.

18. Channeling & Automatic writing: these are much the same except in the output form. Often channeling is spoken aloud, recorded on video or heard in a room full of people like Darryl Anka channeling Bashar or Esther Hick channeling Abraham Hicks. Automatic writing is channel while writing or drawing the words or images. You can channel any being - humans, entities, Aliens, Spirits, God, Collective Consciousness…as always be sure to safeguard!

19. Downloading from the fields: this can also be referred to as collective or universal consciousness. As mentioned with the Cosmic Web and Egregore Systems - we can have access to all of these at will but it's a matter of attuning our vibrational resonance to match the level of consciousness that information is in. We do this unintentionally most of the time but the best way to hone it is to practice via meditation - particularly Dr. Joe Dispenza's Brain & Heart Coherence Meditations. Typically, you'll have a ringing sensation in your right ear while downloading.

20. Hypnotherapy: hypnotherapy is the process of closing off the thinking mind and opening the subconscious mind to obtain specific information like past lives, soul contracts, past events, meeting Spirit Guides, angel, & soul family, etc. It's done by a certified practitioner. QHHT (Dolores Cannon) is Quantum Healing Hypnotherapy which is a much deeper form. Do your research and find what will work best for you.

21. Transcendental Meditation: This is a type of meditation where you can transcend space and time and go into 4D and even high states of consciousness. It can be similar to a Kundalini activation but may still differ from person to person.

22. Akashic Records: this is the ancient library style records of everything ever that has happened, what could have happened (multiple timelines & alternative realities) and what will happen.

Ways of Communication

23. Psychedelics: such as Psilocybin mushrooms and DMT can induce altered states of consciousness where you can interact with other interdimensional beings. I'm not a big fan of these as there can sometimes be negative side effects and you could have a "bad trip". We naturally produce DMT in our pineal gland, I feel it's best to go the natural route. To each their own, some people have had incredible experiences with these. Do what you feel is right for yourself and always do your research!

24. Synchronicities: are the MOST common way beings can interact with humans. We live in a holographic matrix that is made up of code. Repeating numbers or Angel numbers can show up regularly when beings / God / the Universe / Guides / Angels are trying to communicate with you. Pay close attention when you see these numbers …

Ways of Communication

25. Messages from Other People: children under 8 (theta brain wave state) and elderly people close to death are typically very open to messages from other dimensions. People who have unlocked their psychic abilities can also bring messages like Psychic Mediums. Sometimes people can have a negative entity attached to them and will act out or even try to attack you in some way if your soul light is too bright to make you move away from them or try to dim your light. You can also be used as a conduit for giving messages to other people as well.

26. Messages from Animals & Plants: just like synchronicities, animals and plants can be signs of interdimensional communication.

27. Dreams, Deja Vu & Day Dreams : pay attention to dreams that feel real, are vivid and have a clear message.

28. OBE: Out of Body Experience are times where you're consciously aware your etheric or astral body has jumped out of your physical body it can be peaceful or frightening. It helps you become aware of your interdimensional bodies and is often life changing.

29. NDE: Near Death Experience are times where you're dead or almost die and are saved. Often your whole life flashes before your eyes and your life's purpose becomes more clear. This also opens psychic abilities.

30. Soul Contracts: you may have soul contracts where you agreed to having contact such as an abduction experience. You're pre-destined to have encounters.

Galactic Etiquette

Just like we have human laws we have to follow, so does our universe- but on a much grander scale. There are "universal police" that regulate and keep watch and punish if and when these aren't followed - which has happened on Earth. Elizabeth April channeled a message about this. Definitely check out her videos on it.

Humans have simple & more complex etiquette we all know about - don't stare, don't point, don't pick your nose in public, etc. Aliens have these too. It's key for us to acknowledge this and use these etiquette tips while contacting them.

Galactic Etiquette

Galactic etiquette is unique to each species. There are thousands of them but when I have interacted with them and what I have learnt from others who also communicate with them one thing is consistent - you must communicate heart centered, from the heart and with passion with clear concise words that you really mean.

Every word, imagine, vibration must have a strong energetic meaning and frequency behind it for it to be fully transmitted. Love is the strongest vibrational resonance we humans have.

Galactic Etiquette

The majority of ET communication is done telepathically. Naturally, the best way to communicate with them is to learn telepathy. Easier said than done. However, it can be done and is a form of communication all humans will eventually learn and become masters of.

We are very high powered beings and have the ability of physically and energetically harming other beings just with our thoughts and vibration. We must be consciously aware of our true selves and our energetic power so we don't unintentionally harm other beings.

How? With practice you'll learn in the next chapter of this book.

Who? Who should you contact first? Ask your Guardian Angel, your Higher Self, Spirit Guides, and Star Family for guidance. They are here for this purpose, to guide you!

Now let's take a deep dive into my Galactic Etiquette tips.

What to Do

- Be kind, courteous and stand in your power
- Master your mind. Know how to calm your mind and control "monkey brain", especially negative thoughts.
- Have clean & cleansed bodies - both physical, spiritual and energetic.
- Clear your karma, heal your trauma, inner child wounding, cleanse out parasites and toxins, clear your mind of low vibrational thoughts and its best to not eat heavy meals at least four hours before contact with little to no meat. Meat can often tether a person into 3D making interdimensional communication more challenging (sometimes for some people - not 100% for everyone).
- Do study human etiquette as many of the traits are about poise and self regulation.
- Know that many types of ETs speak with a continental sounding accent and understand a wide array of languages including English. They can access the human collective consciousness to communicate in your language.
- As mentioned near the beginning, speak with love through your heart center.
- Practice, Practice and practice. Practice with friends, family, take a Vibravision or remote viewing course
- Often times telepathy has exaggerated movements and expressions, try it

Galactic Etiquette

What Not to Do

- Don't freak out! Stay calm and fill your heart with love ♥
- Don't be arrogant, rude, crude and more often than not be serious
- Don't make jokes or talk their ear off at the start (later on as you become more aware and accustom you can loosen up)
- Don't get too excited, fearful, or shocked. This could cause them stress or even harm.
- Don't praise and worship them, we are equals - akin to each other
- Don't treat them like a celebrity or royalty
- Don't lose focus or get distracted
- Don't use slang or swear words
- Don't get upset if they can't answer one of your questions, because of Cosmic Law or safety they may not be able to answer questions regarding timelines, religion, or taking pictures or videos with them

Once you start communicating you can ask them specific questions but these are good general rules to follow at the start.

Practice

Like anything, you must practice doing a new skill to get better at it. Psychic abilities like telepathy and remote viewing use your natural physical and energetic bodies like an organic machine that has muscle memory. If you practice consistently you will build up stronger more well developed abilities - they're just like training your muscles.

1. CE5 Contact
2. Ujjayi Breathing
3. Brain & Heart Coherence Meditation
4. Astral Travel & Lucid Dreaming
5. Remote Viewing
6. Collective Conscious Meditation
7. Simple Contact Meditation
8. Higher Self Connection
9. Merkabah Activation
10. Gratitude
11. Grounding & Chakra clearing
12. Gut brain cleansing.

Practice 1: CE5 ET Contact

Solo or group Oneness Meditations you can listen to and join:

Dr. Steven Greer's CE5 App and Oneness Consciousness Meditations and crop circle tones.

ET Let's Talk Kosta Macreas consciousness contact meditations and world-wide group.

Spiritverse group and mass meditations along with a free full historical and vibrational education series called Spirit Science.

There are many Facebook and online groups that are inclusive and actively do group contact with many resources. You can find my group on Facebook:
CE5 Raising the Global Frequency.

Practice 2: Simplified Ujjayi Breathing

- Inhale and exhale through only your nose
- Keep your mouth closed.
- Constrict your throat to the point that your breathing makes a rushing noise, almost like you're trying to fog up a mirror but with your mouth closed.
- Control your breath with your diaphragm.
- Keep your inhalations and exhalations equal in duration.
- Close one nostril while breathing in and the other while breathing out.
- Do this for 5-10 minutes then breathe normally.

This can be calming and balancing.
At first, it may feel like you're not getting enough air, but the technique should become easier with practice.

This is a very simplified version to give you an idea of it. There are so many excellent guided videos on YouTube that explain it completely by breathwork masters. If you have the opportunity to do an in-person breathing workshop it's well worth it.

Practice 3: Brain & Heart Coherence

Dr. Joe Dispenza's brain & heart coherence meditations are the gateway into 5th dimensional consciousness. I have used his meditations for many years to heal my body, low self esteem, clear my fears, and heartaches.

I found that doing these meditations daily for at least 3 months is a sure way into 5D consciousness - with all the bonuses of obtaining brain & heart coherence. Such as, lengthening of the telomeres (DNA lifeline extends your life). The ultra-healing natural chemical release of serotonin, DMT, oxytocin and more, ability to release stuck energy in the body relieving pain and helps to clear away disease. The brain & heart are in perfect rhythm for repairing and evolving the full body.

You can find his meditations and hundreds of testimonials on YouTube and his website: https://drjoedispenza.com/

Practice 4: Lucid Dreaming and Astral Travel

These Astral travel methods are very similar except for how you get into the astral state.
Lucid dreaming is when you are in a dream and you become conscious and take control of your dream.
Astral travel is when you are able to consciously relax your body and move your energetic Astral body out.
There are plenty of different ways to get into these states but the ones I have found most effective to be are:
Lucid dreaming: look at your hands multiple times a day (10-15 times) consciously and loudly say "when I look at my hands I become aware".

Do this everyday and topically after 2-4 nights you'll look at them in your dream. That's your cue to realize you're dreaming. You can fly anywhere, think of anything and make it instantly manifest. You can travel to almost anywhere and even interact with other beings.

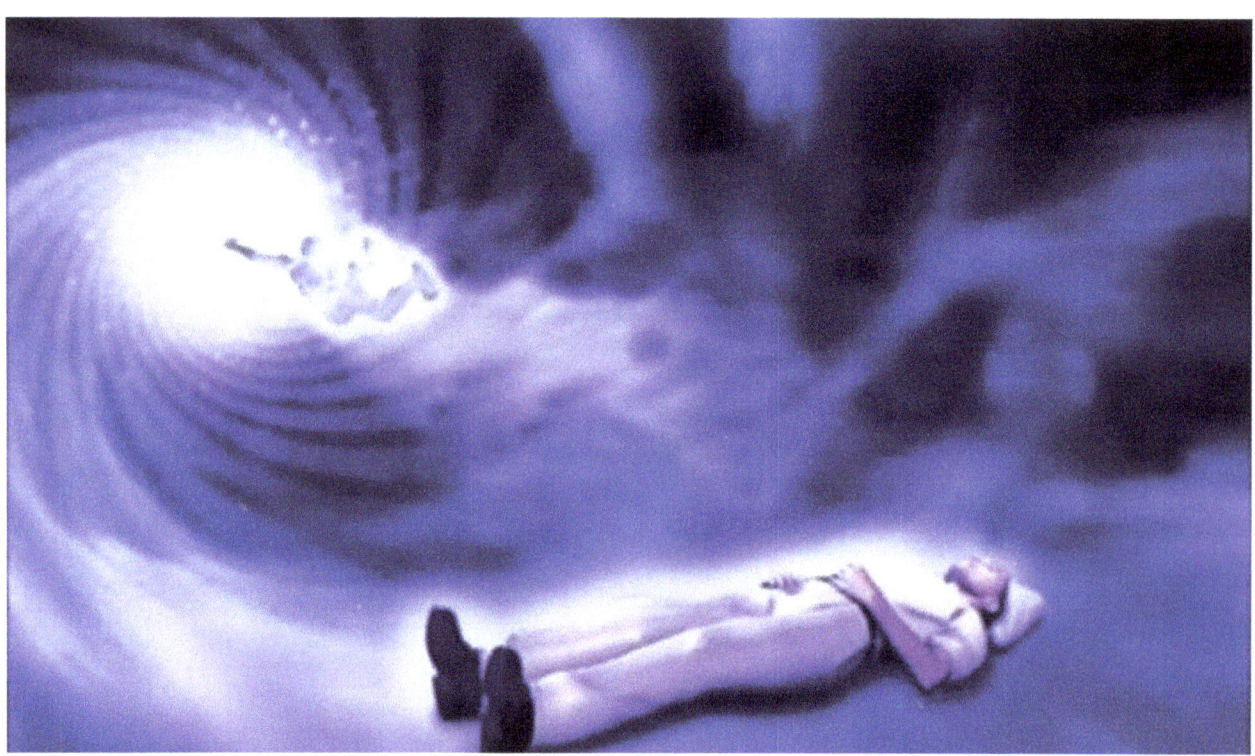

Practice 5: Remote Viewing

As mentioned earlier in this book is also called telesthesia, remote sensing and similar to bi-location – The ability to see and/or a distant or unseen target using extrasensory perception. (Wikipedia, 2023). This isn't just "woowoo airy fairy" practice. At its highest level, it's very structured and has been heavily scientifically studied for many decades. Just look into the CIA's Stargate Project and view the link below for their full RSV instructions.

There are plenty of exceptional free and paid remote viewing courses online, it's best to take a course and research into it as much as you can before attempting it. There are a few different ways you can go about it - more or less scientifically structured. For me, I rely on my Clairvoyant and other Clair abilities to remote view and sense objects, people, places and events. Here are my course recommendations:

- The Farsight Institute: https://farsight.org/SRV/index.html
- CIA's Remote Viewing Protocols:
- https://www.cia.gov/readingroom/docs/CIA-RDP96-00789R002200070001-0.pdf
- Monroe Institute: https://www.monroeinstitute.org/products/remote-viewing
- Dr. Steven Greer's DVD RV course https://shop.siriusdisclosure.com/

There are tons of resources online for learning this amazing and fun skill. As we ascend this will be an extremely important skill to have.

Practice 6: Collective Consciousness Activations & Reprogramming Meditation

See Brian Scott's YouTube video on the Collective Consciousness Activation & Healing Meditation. https://www.youtube.com/watch?v=pfiZOx9HJI4

In order for humanity to take the next consciousness leap forward we all have to be awake and on the same level collectively. Every human's ascension soul journey is important. As you individually ascend, you're helping many other humans too. So people in lower vibrations can bring humanity down. The upside is that positive benevolence is much more powerful than low vibes.

Humans are exceptional at raising the vibration of energy up so high it transmutes low vibes! As a lightworker, this is a massive part of the lightworker soul journey.

Happy light working ✨

Practice 7: Simple Contact Meditation

Finish whatever pertinent things you need to do. If any thoughts come into your mind or reminders. Let your body and mind know, you will do it later so nothing will take your mind off of your breath.

Sit on the floor in the middle of your home or room or bed. Get centered with your surroundings. Roll your shoulders back and neck side to side while taking in deep breaths in through your nose and out your mouth.

Let out a big sigh three times. Take deep breaths in through your nose and out through your mouth with a gentle sigh. Set your intention, who do you want to contact? Your Star Family, Spirit Guides, Ancestors, Loved ones, Jesus, God?

Connect your Earth Star Chakra into the center sun and connect your Soul Star Chakra into Source (see Light Body diagrams). Connect into your Higher Self (Your 5D+ Self). Look around with your 3rd eye - what or who do you see? What do you hear, taste, smell, feel?

It may take time to see or sense anything or it may happen instantly. No matter what, practice is key.

Happy contacting

Practice 8: Higher Self Connection

How to connect to your higher self and why?

Your Higher Self is essentially your future self in at least two or more ascension levels ahead. So as a 3D human your Higher Self would be your 5D self. If you're 5D activated, you can connect with your 7D self as well as other dimensional selves. You can book a session with me for one on one training and feedback.

Or, listen to Brian Scott's Higher Self Meditation is a great first step:
https://www.youtube.com/watch?v=OapgsuYc1r0

Why connect

It's another safeguard way of making sure you're connecting with 5D+ benevolent beings. Low vibrational beings won't be able to come close to you in your Higher Self Connection as they will be instantly transmuted back into Source ✨

Practice 9: Merkaba Activation

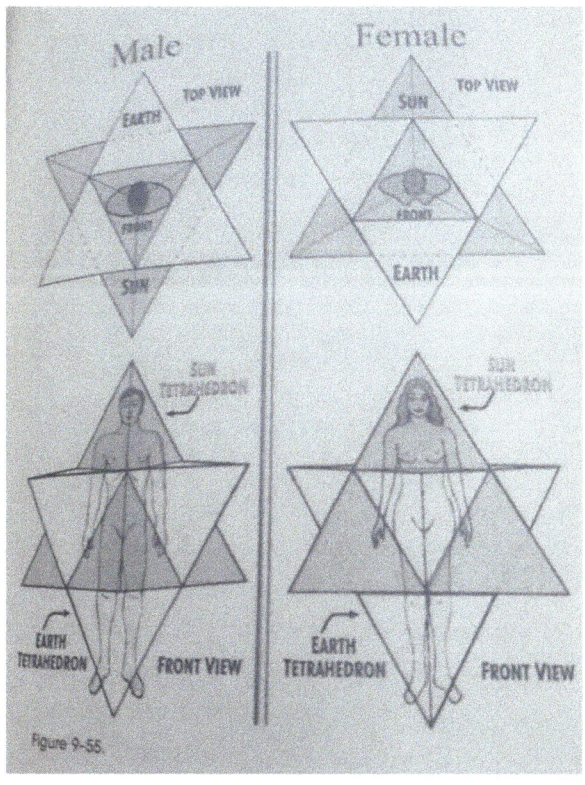

Note that the male and female Merkabas have equal & opposite directions

The Merkabah is an activation of the full light body vessel. As you can see it differs between biological males and females. Female energy is giving while male energy is taking. If you're not sure of your gender, this will make it very difficult to activate - which is another reason why this is hidden, shamed and we're programmed to be confused about gender from a young age. This is an incredibly powerful activation where we can instantly manifest, travel vast distances, do instant healing, and obtain what humans call "miracles" or "super hero" abilities. This has been said to be a key piece of what humans need to activate during the three days of darkness to help make our transition to 5D crystalline bodies with more ease.

Brian Scott has exceptional YouTube videos, especially meditations. Not only have they helped to heal and transform me but they're helping millions all over the world. I highly recommend his Merkabah activation meditation here:
https://www.youtube.com/watch?v=ID3ai77USiw

You can also search online for other Merkabah activation videos - there are many. What might work for some people may not work for everyone, as we're all different.

Practice 10
Gratitude

Practicing gratitude is so simple but creates massive change and abundance in life. The impact can be enormous! Here are my top gratitude exercises:

Say these out loud every morning:

I love and approve of myself
I honor myself, I value myself
I appreciate myself, I am happy
I honor myself, I am worthy
I am safe, healthy & abundant

Say these outloud everyday for 21 days, at that point you will begin to rewire your neurological pathways and your DNA to match the vibration of the words (Billy Carson).

Personal Tip: pick something out on/about a person, thing, plant or animal, or something in your vicinity to compliment and be thankful for.

I used to do this all the time, as a kid I was really shy and often people made me nervous. I often felt out of place, like an inconvenience, and unhappy. I'm not sure where I learnt it but I started complimenting people in my mind - "that person has a nice smile, that person has a beautiful shirt, that person looks like they have hilarious stories!" I'd think nice thoughts about each person I came into contact with. After a couple weeks of doing this, people started smiling at me all the time. It was like my mind and energy shifted to a higher gratitude vibration and people could feel it.

In my early 20s, I started listening to and reading up on Louise Hay. Especially her book 'You Can Heal Your Life'. It was Life changing, being grateful for everything also helped to open up my psychic abilities, remove negative attachments and helped to stop the psychic attacks I was getting - along with yoga and music. It helped to raise my vibration and in turn helped me to positively affect others around me.

Try this out, next time you go anywhere shoot love and compliments at people in your mind and see their reactions. It's amazing to see how subtle positive energy vibes can positively impact people on an energetic level.

Practice 11
Chakra Clearing & Activation

Chakras are the energetic centers that each layer of your energy bodies connects into.

Sit on the floor in the middle of your home or in a place you feel comfortable - you can sit on a chair if need be.

Starting at the bottom then moving upward, imagine each chakra as a spinning jewel. It spins slowly clockwise then starts to go faster and any dark spots get lighter and lighter until it's a pure vibrant color.

Red at the base, orange at the sacral, yellow at the solar plexus, green at the heart, bright blue in the throat, deep indigo blue in the third eye pineal gland, violet for the top crown chakra. Strengthen your connection to them and to clearing them each day. Once you're comfortable add on your other many chakras including the ear, hands, finger tips, feet, soul and earth stars and many others shown in this book.

Inner Child Healing

Imagine you're a kid again, maybe 7 or 10 years old. A memorable time for you. You're in your bedroom. What would you tell yourself? Advice you would give yourself? If you feel the need, apologize and forgive for things no matter what happened. Forgive, say sorry and release any stuck energy or emotions. Hug and comfort yourself as a child, give words of encouragement. Tell yourself you love them and are with them.

Not only can this provide great inner child healing, it can also re-write the Quantum. 3D Time-Space is part of the matrix system. In higher dimensions, time space is happening much faster and you can access many different time spaces to view and sometimes interact with. Our future and past selves can energetically affect

Shadow Work

This is when you review the darkest parts of yourself, your past, and purge through often what's referred to as "A Dark Night of the Soul". This will help to clear your chakras and make you less dense.

Practice 12

Gut Mind Cleansing

Always consult with a certified professional before trying anything.

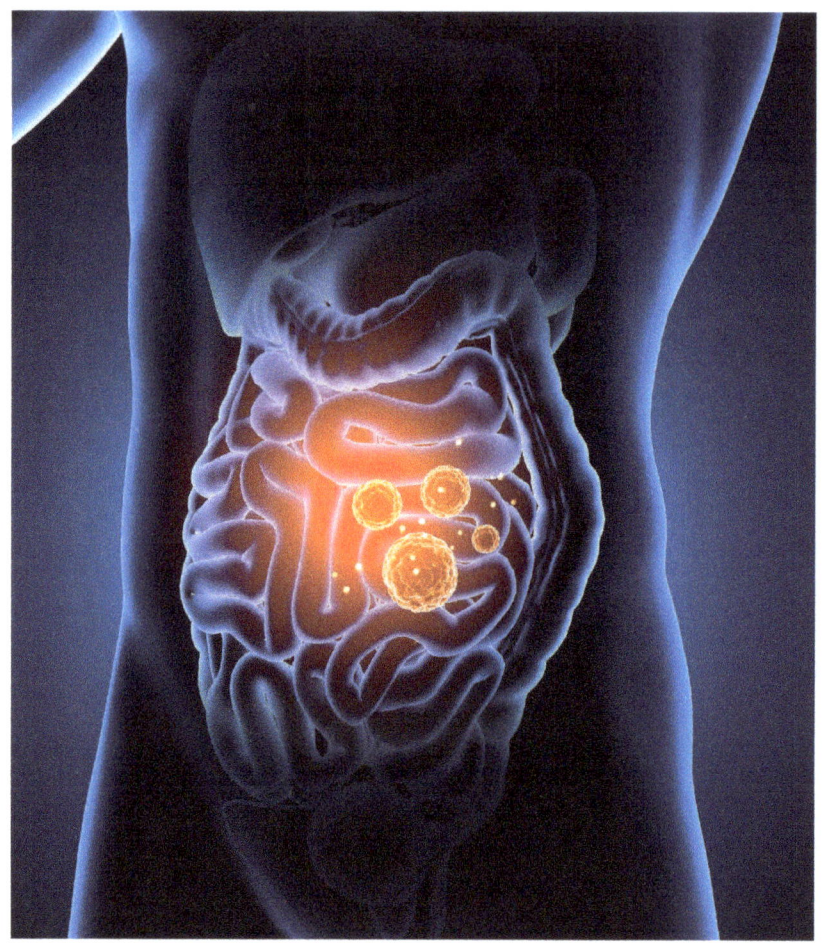

Start simple with intermittent fasting and by doing a simple salt water cleanse.

First, clear your day, don't work, no appointments. Just chill at home. Mix 4 cups of warm water with 2 teaspoons of pink Himalayan salt or pure sea salt. Make sure the salt is fully dissolved. Chug it. Stay close by the bathroom and within 20-30 minutes you will be flushing out.

Meditate, journal, reflect, practice forgiveness and gratitude. It's a great time to do Vagus Nerve exercises to release, calm and ground your whole system.

Research cleanses online, find what's right for you, and find a specialist to get advice from. Other options are: charcoal, spirulina, juices, teas, and herbs.

(Note: I am not a doctor or trained nutritionist, always consult with a medical professional prior to altering your diet or doing a cleanse.)

Resources

My first book 5D Consciousness Activations showcases much more vital information and resources. For now, search and review each of these resources for more information on Star Beings, world events, remote viewing insights and galactic disclosure. In no particular order:

1. ET Let's Talk - Kosta Macreas
2. Elizabeth April
3. Dr. Joe Dispenza
4. Louise Hay
5. Spirit Science
6. 4Bidden Knowledge - Billy Carson
7. Exopolitics - Dr. Michael Salla
8. Sirius Disclosure - Dr. Steven Greer
9. David Wilcock
10. Corey Goode
11. Emery Smith
12. The Farsight Institute & Farsight Prime
13. MUFON
14. Sam the Illusionist
15. Alex Collier
16. Gaia
17. Sharma Pillay
18. Akasha Awakened - Kayla Koivisto
19. Dolores Cannon
20. Journey of Souls - Michael Newton
21. Darryl Anka channeling Bashar
22. The Experiencer Support Association - Ryan Stacey
23. The Reality Revolution - Brian Scott
24. UNIFYD TV - Jason Shurka
25. RA - the Law of One
26. 4D University - Aaron Abke
27. Next Level Soul Podcast - Alex Ferrari
28. Mindvalley - Vishen Lakhiani
29. ECETI Ranch - James Gilliland
30. Doenut Factory
31. Abraham Hicks via Esther Hicks
32. Apocrypha
33. The Books of Enoch, Thomas, Mary, & Joseph
34. The Dead Sea Scrolls & Epic of Gilgamesh
35. Vibravision

Image Page Links

- 0.2, 0.1, 2 Canva stock photos
- 3 https://medium.com/@kuhujakhmola123/cord-cutting-meditation-steps-and-benefits-114b68a5e2a1
- 4 https://thewishingtrees.com/blog/the-manifestation-masterstroke-part-2/
- 7, 8, 9 Canva created images with stock photos
- 10 https://christosavatar.com/
- 11 https://www.instagram.com/p/CFAScTuHo3z/?igshid=10w2egw7uo5m4&epik=dj0yJnU9TkVUdmV6UWYxbGO5YlJCX0tCUkxGeHE4bHczZlFjUDMmcD0wJm49cVVqdUFudGJWR1FWZmUzZldrdmhfQSZ0PUFBQUFBR1FLWEY4
- 12 https://awakentothebeyond.com/writings/
- 13 https://www.reddit.com/r/lawofone/comments/n23m8t/the_7_densities_of_consciousness/
- 14 https://umamaya.com/classical-tarot-akashic-reading/
- 15 https://primalalchemy.co.uk/collections/ascension-maps
- 16 https://beingoflight.brotherofyeshua.com/
- 17 https://sdsu-physics.org/physics180/physics180B/Topics/electromagnetism/electrowaves.html
- 18 https://www.once.lighting/en/news/the-visible-light-spectrum
- 18 https://www.pinterest.ca/pin/555068722794285676/
- 19 https://www.quora.com/What-is-Kundalini-meditation-and-how-is-it-done
- 20 https://www.pinterest.ca/pin/701787554453619458/
- 21 https://livingenlightenedrelationships.com/activations/the-crystal-shift-becoming-the-crystalline-human/
- 22 https://www.pinterest.ca/pin/835136324637711360/
- 23 https://yourbodyhastheanswer.com/palm-chakras/palm-chakras/
- 23 https://medium.com/@nitinpedia17/hand-mudras-in-yoga-practice-0ac2eebe56d6
- 24 https://www.pinterest.ca/pin/669910513320598670/
- 24 https://www.fitsri.com/articles/how-to-awaken-kundalini
- 25 https://mind-matrix.net/the-ascension/the-mind-matrix-kingdoms/multi-dimensional-realities/19-ra-law-of-one/
- 27 https://www.pinterest.ca/pin/309552174363460258/
- 27 https://www.vashta.com/my-product_category/commisions/
- 27 https://www.deviantart.com/eugenius330/art/Reptilian-Being-1800x3200-565919975
- 27 https://goldenageofgaia.com/2021/03/23/mira-from-the-pleiadian-high-council-new-energies-and-timelines/
- 27 https://www.abovetopsecret.com/forum/thread1193777/pg1
- 27 https://meredithwalters.com/real-reason-you-cant-do-what-others-can/
- 30 https://www.pinterest.ca/pin/70437487281601/
- 32 https://www.pinterest.ca/pin/997828861176131692/
- 33 https://www.pablocarlosbudassi.com/2021/02/the-infographic-and-artistic-work-named.html
- 33 https://www.pinterest.ca/pin/70437487281601/
- 35 https://monatomic-orme.com/what-is-sacred-geometry-and-how-can-it-help-you/
- 36, 37, 39 Canva stock photos
- 42 https://etherealsoul.net/blog/the-oversoul-and-higher-self-of-the-soul-explained/
- 43 Canva stock photo
- 47 https://za.pinterest.com/pin/294563631868461021/
- 48 https://higherdensity.wordpress.com/2013/05/02/your-voice-commands-your-mind-body-spirit/
- 49 https://www.pinterest.ca/pin/701928291902259685/
- 50 https://reikilifestyle.com/
- 52 https://awakeningtimes.com/the-physics-of-consciousness-the-zero-point-field-pineal-gland-and-out-of-body-experience/
- 52 https://scienceinfo.net/decipher-the-mysterious-phenomenon-the-soul-leaves-the-body.html
- 53 https://www.pinterest.ca/pin/777152479428840957/
- 53 https://shop.siriusdisclosure.com/pages/ce5-contact-app
- 55 https://www.pinterest.ca/pin/160370436724063712/
- 56 https://themindsjournal.com/animals-as-omens/
- 57 https://harley-has-wilson.blogspot.com/2022/04/the-laws-of-universe-pdf.html
- 58 https://www.sangeetahanda.net/post/july-26th-the-sirian-earth-new-year
- 60 https://anomalien.com/was-jesus-an-extraterrestrial-or-possibly-an-anunnaki-hybrid/
- 61 https://secretenergy.com/how-to-raise-your-vibration-before-going-to-sleep/
- 62, 63, 64, 66, 67, 68, 69 Canva stock photos
- 65 https://www.pinterest.de/pin/331577591307234452/
- 70 http://www.angeliquelarson.com/blog/the-light-body-sacred-geometric-activation
- 70 https://www.pinterest.es/pin/pin-de-ann-em--1970393578075122/
- 72 & 73 Canva stock photos

About the Author

LMM with 5D Life Now is a contactee, abductee and experiencer of many different types of Cosmic and Terrestrial beings. She had contact from a very young age and throughout her life. She didn't know what really happened as a child until in her 30s she got a major wake up call when two Reptilian beings showed up in her room. You can hear about her experiences and expansive cosmic knowledge on her website 5dlifenow.co, YouTube and TikTok @5DLIFENOW.

She is also a CE5 host, Clairvoyant Mystic and yoga & music enthusiast. She does Mystic Higher Self sessions by request where she connects through Higher Self connection.

Earlier in her life, she went to Catholic school and was raised by fairly strict Christian parents. From the age of seven, she became consciously aware that there was much more going on in this reality than everyone was aware of. She made a decision in that moment to dedicate a secret life mission to figuring out what was actually happening here. And, she did!

Be sure to subscribe to her email list on her website 5dlifenow.co for the launch dates. You can book her for events, conferences, workshops and interviews here: 5dlifenow@gmail.com

About the Author

5D Consciousness Activations and The Top 15 5D Consciousness Activations are published on her website and on Amazon. This is an excellent booklet for beginners and teachers that are looking for simple easy to read graphs and diagrams about 5D consciousness.

Here are some of her next booklets to be released in the future:

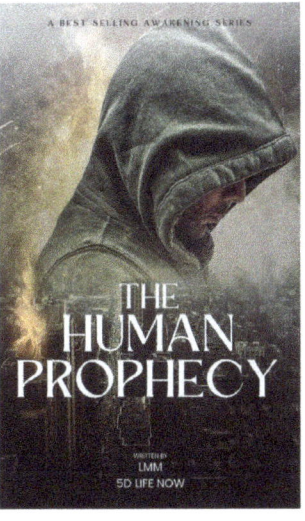

www.ingramcontent.com/pod-product-compliance
Lightning Source LLC
LaVergne TN
LVHW070533070526
838199LV00075B/6772